BEING CHRISTIAN

A UNITED METHODIST VISION
FOR THE CHRISTIAN LIFE

*Based on John Wesley's Original Tract
"The Character of a Methodist"*

JERRY L. MERCER

DISCIPLESHIP RESOURCES
MATERIALS FOR GROWTH IN CHRISTIAN FAITH & LIFE
NASHVILLE, TENNESSEE

❖ **TO PLACE AN ORDER** OR TO INQUIRE ABOUT RESOURCES AND CUSTOMER ACCOUNTS, CONTACT:

DISCIPLESHIP RESOURCES DISTRIBUTION CENTER
P.O. BOX 6996
ALPHARETTA, GEORGIA 30239-6996

TEL: (800) 685-4370

FAX: (404) 442-5114

❖   ❖   ❖

❖ **FOR EDITORIAL INQUIRIES** AND RIGHTS AND PERMISSIONS REQUESTS, CONTACT:

DISCIPLESHIP RESOURCES EDITORIAL OFFICES
P.O. BOX 840
NASHVILLE, TENNESSEE 37202-0840

TEL: (615) 340-7068

Cover design by Tim Hornbeak.

Unless otherwise indicated, all scripture quotations are taken from the New Revised Standard Version of the Holy Bible. Copyright © 1989 by the Division of Christian Education of the National Council of Churches of Christ in the USA and used by permission.

Library of Congress Catalog Card No. 93-72074

ISBN 0-88177-125-2

DR125

To

MAXINE AND V. V.

FOR LIFE

AND

LENORA AND DON

FOR RUTH

CONTENTS

Preface

Early one summer evening the noise level in our kitchen was rising by the minute. A couple of our daughters and their husbands had dropped by for a visit. As usual, the conversation flew thick and fast around the table. Then Robert, the first of my sons-in-law, said he had an announcement to make. Gradually everyone quieted down. "I've been thinking about this for a long time," he said, "and I want to become a United Methodist." Then turning to me, he continued, "But I don't know what to do. Will you lead me?"

Naturally I felt very happy. For over thirty years I have served The Methodist and then The United Methodist Church as a pastor. The United Methodist Church was formed in 1968 as the result of the union of the former Methodist and Evangelical United Brethren Churches. My wife, Ruth, has been active in the church since her childhood. Each of our four daughters was baptized and raised as a Methodist Christian. The Methodist tradition has shaped our family life and our values. Robert was also raised as a Christian, but in a church vastly different from ours. Although we honored Robert's previous commitments without question, Ruth and I were thrilled with his announcement. This was a big step for him to take, and, as I was to discover, for me, too!

As other members of the family cheered him on, I began to think what I would do. How could I possibly convey to Robert what The United Methodist Church is about and do it in a way that would not overwhelm him? I asked myself, What is the first thing he needs to know as he anticipates membership? What is most important for him now? Then it came to me: Help Robert catch the Methodist spirit! He could learn about our history later, and he would discover how the church functioned as he worked with it. If I could help him rub shoulders with John Wesley's own excitement about what it means to be "altogether a Christian," perhaps that would do it. Thus my plan became to introduce my son-in-law to the dream that the early Methodists shared with Wesley: that *God's love makes willing people happy and fulfilled.*

I then easily decided what to do next. For years I have been sharing with various United Methodist congregations the contents of a small tract John Wesley considered one of the most important he ever wrote: "The Character of a Methodist." (This tract and a paraphrase are printed in full in Appendices A and B.) For over forty years of Wesley's ministry this ten-paragraph statement represented the heart of his concern for a fully loving and fully obedient Christian people. In fact, it was so important to him that Wesley included it in a much larger paper he wrote on *Christian perfection*, a term Wesley used to describe his understanding of God's love alive in the hearts of serious Christians. As I saw it, "The Character of a Methodist" would be the window through which I hoped Robert would see something of the spiritual vitality of our church and discover what that energy could mean for him and for his family.

Over the next several months I wrote a series of letters to Robert, one on each of the ten paragraphs of Wesley's tract. In these letters I shared something of what Wesley called "the grand design" that God had in mind "for the people called Methodist." I quickly discovered that the letters encouraged me as well, as I looked once again at the roots of my own faith and the genius of my spiritual tradition. As I wrote to Robert, the living connection between the early Methodists and the church today became increasingly clear to me. We both wanted the same thing: a vital and meaningful faith. Thus "The Character of a Methodist" not only introduced Robert to our church but it reaffirmed the meaning of Methodism in my own life.

One must realize that the life Wesley described is more of an agenda for spiritual growth than a statement of an accomplished fact. For this reason I try to keep some balance in this book between dream and reality. Wesley put before us a *vision of excellence*. The goals of our spiritual walk are high; there is no disputing that. Yet they are goals that coax us, draw us — not goals that threaten or drive us. They say to us, regardless of the level of our faith, "Come up higher." The Methodist movement has always believed that all of life is enhanced by God's love. And love attracts; it does not force. You will be reading correctly if these chapters prompt you to reflect on your own life and help you see ways you can be more open to God's love.

This book is a reworking of my letters to Robert. Ruth and I decided to edit and expand them and to share their contents with you. We believe that no matter whether you are looking at The United Methodist Church with the thought of joining, whether you are one of its long-standing members, or whether you are simply interested in knowing the characteristics of true Christianity from Wesley's perspective, Wesley's spiritual insight will cause your heart, as was Wesley's, to be "strangely warmed." You will sense and participate in Wesley's dream for a vibrant, caring faith, begun in this life in the company of the church and completed later in the kingdom of God. And we are quite sure you will be glad you met "the people called Methodist."

My sincere appreciation to Craig Gallaway, Editorial Director for Discipleship Resources, and David Hazlewood, Publisher, for their encouragement and support. Their efforts, combined with the constant and gentle nudging of my wife Ruth, have brought the book to completion. In addition, the assistance of my co-workers, Carolyn Smith and Sheryl Voigts, and the efforts of J. Lee Bonnet and Kathy Manor in Nashville have been invaluable to me. My readers will especially appreciate their work! The research for the book was partially done on a sabbatical provided by my school, Asbury Theological Seminary. To God be the glory!

One

HAPPINESS

From the time we drew our first breath, all we have wanted from life is happiness. John Wesley believed that happiness is our natural number one priority. Senators, homemakers, executives, assembly-line workers, and pastors — like everyone else — long for it. Of course, what is required to give us a sense of well-being depends on our age and circumstance. At first we were quite satisfied to have a full stomach and a dry diaper. But as adults our happiness may require a sense of status in the community or the surge of power from the car we drive. But whatever else we may want for ourselves, we want to attain happiness — an inner confidence that life is good.

For years I have asked people what would make them really happy. I have yet to hear anyone say, "I don't know." We all have opinions about what will make us happy. On one occasion a man told me, "If I could just communicate with my wife, I would be very happy." "Happy," she replied, "if my child could get off drugs. . . ." A young couple laughed, "Well, if we could have some money left over after the bills are paid, maybe enough to take a vacation or at least buy some clothes." A young wife quipped, "Happiness, that's easy; not to be plagued with unwanted advice from my in-laws." Of all the answers I have received across the years, the top three are peace in the family, meaningful work, and a vital faith. Each of us longs for a peaceful life, especially among family members, and a sense that we are doing something worthwhile with our lives.

Being happy is not easy, especially when we consider the extent of the unhappiness around us. Feelings of unhappiness are widespread, and the reasons for them are difficult to identify. Traditional theologians attribute the cause to original sin, while contemporary theologians consider unhappiness a result of the misuse of our God-given freedom. Anthropologist Earnest Becker, not a religious person himself, thinks most Westerners have lost a sense of meaning because they have lost "all belief in spiritual causality."[1] Becker says our society has largely replaced confidence in God with confidence in technology. We tend to interpret our place in the universe on the basis of scientific achievement. We devise long lists of things to blame for the void in our lives: if we only had better laws, better education, better job opportunities, better spouses, better children, better working conditions . . . we could settle back and be happy. But even these things do not prevent many of us from turning to drugs, alcohol, and indulgence as quick ways to feel good — to be happy.

We seem to want what we cannot have or cannot find. Wesley recognized that many people look for happiness where it cannot be found. Perhaps when we have exhausted all other avenues, we discover that happiness is the gift of God.

A LEGACY OF HAPPINESS

What is this happiness Wesley spoke of? It is "the way of pleasantness; the path to calm, joyous peace."[2] In a more recent idiom, we speak of meaning in life or a sense of fulfillment. For Wesley, words such as *joy, happiness, blessedness,* and *love* are all interchangeable. These certainly do not describe a trite happiness as we see so often when these words are used today. The happiness Wesley wanted his followers to know is the gift of God. In fact, it is the life of God in our souls. This concept may become clearer as we think about three words: *creation, grace,* and *recreation.*

CREATION. Interpreting the creation narrative in Genesis, Wesley concluded that human beings were created for "eternal continuance" in both a happy and a holy life. The story is a familiar one. Adam and Eve were placed in a paradise of goodness and satisfaction, but they lost their place through disobedience.[3] We, too, are brought into the world with a freedom and a yearning to do God's will. But we misuse our freedom, as they did, and, as a result, live frustrated lives. However, the positive side to this frustration is that no matter how deep our problems are, we can realize we were created to reflect God's love and goodness. Even though we may botch God's intention for us in creation, we can be re-created in Christ!

GRACE. This beautiful word speaks of a God of boundless love, a God of mercy who delights in showing favor to those who turn to God for help.[4] Grace is absolutely free to those who ask for it, with no requirement except faith in Christ and a desire to turn from the wrong they have done. What else need we hear, we who so often feel unloved and unworthy, who tend to look at ourselves as failures and phonies? Our failure to live up to God's expectations is taken up in God's abundant mercy, and we who were estranged from God are now God's delight.[5]

RECREATION. For Wesley, Christians are not just improved people, they are new people! "So if anyone is in Christ, there is a new creation: everything old has passed away; see, everything has become new" (2 Corinthians 5:17).[6] Wesley understood the Apostle Paul to say that Christ has power to radically alter our basic sense of who we are. Wesley used words such as *new life*, *new affections* (desires), *new ideas*, and *new conceptions* to describe what he meant.[7] We can believe then that Christ gives us a sense of freshness, a new start, and empowers us to love what is good, peaceful, and true. This is nothing less than seeing the world through new eyes! One cannot possibly miss Wesley's meaning. We who are sinners are being restored by and to God's awesome love, a love in which we can walk the rest of our days. This is the reason Methodists can be happy. They are happy because, to them, God is like an ever-flowing fountain, constantly cleansing, healing, and bringing them toward wholeness.

THE WAR ZONE

This kind of happiness is not, however, blind optimism. The world in which we seek to be happy is as full of terror as it is of tranquility. Social scientists and artists never tire of reminding us that we live surrounded by human evil. All we need do is watch the news broadcasts to realize how right they are. In fact, so much confusion and threat exist in our world that we may be tempted to respond like Dr. Rieux, the no-nonsense humanist physician of Albert Camus' novel, *The Plague*. Overwhelmed by the human wreckage caused by a fierce plague (Camus' symbol for war), a tired Rieux complains that "the order of the world is shaped by death."[8] Death everywhere! Misery everywhere! Life is a battlefield!

Reflecting on the dilemmas of life, psychologist Erich Fromm says our natural need for a sense of order and purpose is framed by both "life-furthering" and "life-strangling" passions.[9] The demoniacs of the New Testament are frightening reminders that human experience then and now is subject to appetites for cruelty and destructiveness of every sort. I heard the story of a man who said that for much of his life he awoke every morning looking for someone to hate. His pathology was lived out in a motorcycle gang known for random, sadistic violence. When I heard this fellow, he was speaking as a

Christian, as one who had made the difficult journey from "life-strangling" to "life-furthering" passions. Unlike Rieux, this man saw the order of life as well as the order of death working in nature. And like a certain demoniac, he now sat at the feet of Jesus, "clothed and in his right mind" (Luke 8:26-39).

Wesley did not expect naive happiness in his followers. The Christians of his day lived in a culture victimized by a "flood of unrighteousness and ungodliness."[10] In his sermon "National Sins and Miseries," Wesley launched a frontal attack on the social corruption that ravaged the poor, dehumanized children, and justified slavery. He realized that happiness must be carved out of a giant stone of resistance. Happiness consists of satisfaction with life lived under the most unsatisfying conditions and of a determination to speak of goodness and growth to a society steeped in suspicion and fear. One can easily understand why Wesley sometimes described life as a war zone between great and terrible powers.[11]

In the happiness section of "The Character" one finds a hint of the paradox Christians face when evil seems to be winning the day. This paradox is hidden in Psalm 73 from which Wesley drew ideas to express the depth of joy one can have in God. Toward the end of the psalm the writer muses:

> *Whom have I in heaven but you?*
> *And there is nothing on earth*
> *that I desire other than you.*
> *My flesh and my heart may fail,*
> *but God is the strength of my*
> *heart and my portion forever (25-26).*

Although that exclamation of faith is tremendous and uplifting, the psalm actually begins on an anxious and questioning note. The dilemma of the psalmist stems from his growing suspicion that God favors the wicked more than the righteous; after all, it is the wicked who have all the riches and power, and he, the psalmist, has nothing! The psalmist had been taught that God deals harshly with the wicked, but in verses 3-16 he describes the wicked prospering while they manipulate others. Indeed, they openly scoff at God. Unable to make sense of this, the psalmist lashes out, lamenting that God is punishing Israel unfairly. The verses Wesley quoted come later in the psalm after the psalmist has had a change of heart.

Two key statements in Psalm 73 help us understand the marvelous verses used by Wesley. The first is in verses 2-3:

> *. . . as for me, my feet had almost stumbled;*
> *my steps had nearly slipped.*
> *For I was envious of the arrogant;*
> *I saw the prosperity of the wicked.*

The psalmist assumed that God was far away and that something was wrong with his faith. "When I thought how to understand this," he mused, "it seemed to me a wearisome task" (verse 16).

The second pivotal statement is in verse 17:

> *. . . I went into the sanctuary of God;*
> *then I perceived their end.*

When the psalmist went to the Temple, something happened. Although his circumstances did not change, his heart did.

God granted him insight into what became a recurring biblical theme: the ultimate downfall of the wicked. In verse 2, it was the psalmist who was about to stumble; in verse 18, the psalmist now knows the wicked will finally stumble. Righteousness will be vindicated, though not necessarily in this life.

Now this is exactly what Wesley meant by happiness. Life is good in spite of its many perplexing problems. We may be bloodied in the battle, but God will bring us through to victory. Genuine faith does not gloss over the difficulties and seeming inequities that Christians face; there are many loose ends to contend with, and it is not always possible to track the steps of God. But when the issues are of life and death, the gospel is trustworthy. In Christ peace will triumph. Wesley was schooled in a spirituality that cautioned against expecting too much from life's situations. On the other hand, putting our complete trust in God enables us to rejoice with those who rejoice, to weep with those who weep, and to cope with those who stand against us. To be happy in God is to "fight the good fight," as the Apostle Paul said, and to know that the day belongs to the Lord.

A DANCING HEART

Emerson wrote, that "in the mud and scum of things . . . something always sings."[12] For the poet, that something may have been "the redbreast's mellow tone," but for the English revival it was the rousing song of hearts set free. When "joy is full" and "all our bones cry out," as Wesley said, praise becomes the language of the spirit.

And praise the early Methodists did! Charles Wesley penned an estimated 6,000 hymns and spiritual songs to help grateful souls express their experience and hope.

One of the sections in *Collection of Hymns for the Use of the People Called Methodists* is titled "For Believers Rejoicing." Imagine what it must have been like on a warm afternoon to hear a thousand or more joy-filled people lift this song to heaven.

> *My God, I am thine; What a comfort divine,*
> *What a blessing to know that my Jesus is mine!*
> *In the heavenly Lamb Thrice happy I am,*
> *And my heart it doth dance at the sound of his name.*
>
> *True pleasures abound In the rapturous sound;*
> *And whoever hath found it hath paradise found.*
> *My Jesus to know, And feel his blood flow,*
> *'Tis life everlasting, 'tis heaven below!* [13]

On the American frontier, strong emotional experiences among Methodists were as much a part of the campmeeting scenes as were the sermons that sparked them. British Methodism, however, was considerably more restrained than its American counterpart, and Wesley even more so than his followers. In fact, Wesley distrusted emotions — his and anyone else's. But even though he was leery of emotional emphases, he could not keep tears from cutting clean streaks down the dusty cheeks of coalminers as they listened to his sermons at the end of their shifts outside the mine entrance. Wesley had strong feelings, but he had been warned by his readings in spirituality not to trust them too far. But what the Wesley brothers could not release in public spilled over into their hymnody, a hymnody rich in the feelings of faith.

Wesley's own reserve had been strengthened by Thomas à Kempis, the author of the extremely popular devotional classic *The Imitation of Christ*. The writings of this fifteenth century Augustinian monk influenced Wesley and helped fashion his understanding of faith. *The Imitation of Christ*, an austere book, emphasized humility in a manner tailor-made for Wesley's temperament and made an impression on Wesley that he could not shake. What Wesley learned, however, was important for him and for us. Thomas à Kempis did not want persons to place too much importance on their feelings. The danger is that if we don't "feel" religious then we may conclude we are not religious. À Kempis wants his readers to know that God is greater than one's feelings.[14] Wesley took this advice to heart and so should we. Good feelings are wonderful, but they are not always the best indication of what is really going on in our hearts.

In any case, God is the object of our search, not particular feelings. With the living God as your companion, whether you "feel" God or not, then regardless of your circumstances your own heart will "dance at the sound of his name."

METHODISTS: A HAPPY PEOPLE

Common in some places today is the view that religious experience and Christian values are restrictive, even demeaning. Methodists should have a hard time understanding or accepting this attitude. In the Gospel of John we read, "So if the Son makes you free, you will be free indeed" (John 8:36). This good news was the source of early Methodist joy, and history has shown such joy to be contagious. The love of God is not a wearisome burden; it is freedom and true happiness. Through Jesus we have learned that Christian community is not something to be endured; it is a relationship to be cherished and nourished. The sacraments of the church are not formality and legalism; they are ways of experiencing God's abundant grace. The world is not to be abandoned; it is where we are sent with the message of hope.

In their better moments, Methodists have been inspired to faithful living by Wesley's vision of happiness, a vision that is linked with the desire to live an upright life. This means that all of life is hallowed by God's grace, and knowing this gives Christians the deepest satisfaction. To join ranks with the Wesleyan spirit is to identify with a Christian tradition that strives, by the grace of God, to reflect a wholesome life of faith poured out in praise and gratitude to God and in loving service to the human family.

For Reflection and Discussion

1. John Wesley believed that people want to be happy more than anything else. Do you agree with him? Why or why not?

2. The New Testament portrays Christians as a deeply joyous people. In what ways would you describe your life or your congregation as deeply joyous?

3. We often think of Jesus as a man "acquainted with grief." What do you think brought a smile to the face of Jesus?

4. How would you respond to the comment: "Religion takes all the joy out of living"?

Two

HOPE

One would have difficulty finding more devastating words in literature than those inscribed above the Gate of Hell in Dante's *Inferno*. "Through me," the caption reads, is "the way into the suffering city," to "eternal pain." This terrible door opens to the way of "the lost." No wonder those who walk through that door are to "abandon every hope."[1] Thus begins Dante's melancholy descent into the regions of the damned. It is a downward spiral of despondency and desolation. This fantastic poetic creation by the thirteenth-century angry Italian could easily be dismissed as political satire if we did not see its anguish and despair in our own world. *The Inferno* is a troubling symbol of that sense of hopelessness in which many people live today.

Similar seeds of hopelessness were prevalent in Wesley's day. "Abandon every hope, who enter here" could have been the banner waving over the slums where the poorer classes lived in eighteenth-century London. Overcrowded ghettos, exploited workers, and widespread drunkenness were commonplace. Historian Dorothy Marshall says it was "a hard, harsh world for the masses of English people," a world "devoid of pity."[2] A society generally composed of two classes, a few rich and many poor, provided an almost impossible testing-ground for the message of the gospel. We can be thankful that then, as now, the human spirit, no matter how crushed, more often than not turned toward a message of real hope.

Motivated by a dramatic change in his own life, Wesley became an evangelist whose desire was to travel throughout the land broadcasting the possibilities of new life in Christ. Everywhere he went he proclaimed that people were not destined to live in squalor and discouragement but were called to be children of the Most High God. And everywhere he spoke, quite ordinary people, most without influence or wealth, heard that message and were changed from hopelessness to hope.

8

A BIT OF HEAVEN ON EARTH

Commenting on 1 Corinthians 13:13, "And now faith, hope, and love abide, these three; and the greatest of these is love," Wesley writes, "[faith, hope, and love] are the sum of perfection on earth; love alone is the sum of perfection in heaven."[3] Hope is included in the "sum of perfection on earth," because in its New Testament sense, hope never suggests a mere wish or vague anticipation; hope is "always the expectation of something good."[4]

Hope was so important for Wesley that he saw it as a way to gauge the depth of our experience of Christ. If we were to speak with Wesley he would ask us, "Do you have faith in Christ for your salvation?" If we answered *yes*, Wesley would then ask, "Do you believe the Lord who lives in you on earth will receive you in heaven?" If we answered *yes* again, Wesley would respond, "Good! This means you have both faith and hope. You believe in Christ for your present life and for your future life. Always remember, Christ is the content of both faith and hope. Hope is the reality of faith extended into eternity."

This view of hope is expressed in Wesley's sermon, "The Marks of the New Birth."[5] There he underscored his constant refrain that ours is a *living* relationship with God through Christ. The words *new birth*, which Wesley gets from John 3:1-8, suggest that hope is not only something we believe in with our minds but is also a response of our total selves to God. For example, perhaps at one time you thought a particular person could become your best friend. To think that is one thing; it is quite another thing to trust that person with your secrets. Or, to repeat the Apostles' Creed as part of morning worship is good, but to stake one's life on its truth is another matter. Only by God's grace do we invest ourselves in God's future for us. We live by true hope when the matter of our fidelity to God is not debatable. Then our hope is solid, because it is anchored firmly in God's covenant love. Thought of in this way, the content of our hope becomes nothing less than the living God.

Wesley said hope also brings *confidence*. While he did not claim to know how it happens, he believed that the Holy Spirit bears witness within us that our hope in Christ is well placed. While attending the Aldersgate Bible study, he became convinced that Luther's words *about* Christ reflected his experience *of* Christ. Wesley could not prove that God's grace had been given to him; neither could he doubt it. True hope is a gift from God — a gift God is pleased to reveal and to give.

Finally, in "The Marks of the New Birth," Wesley describes hope as something that is secure. When do we tend to become fearful about life? Most often it is when we are suffering, when our lives are racked with emotional or physical pain and things seem to be out of control. How are Christians to face such times? "With confidence," Wesley quickly answers. "When sufferings most abound, the consolation of [God's] Spirit does much more abound."[6] Why doesn't suffering rattle a Christian's basic faith? Because the Christian's hope is in God who comes to us now and forever. Our present suffering is real, but so is the comfort that God gives. Even death cannot shake hope. God's salvation, now and later, is greater than our deepest fears and most painful moments. Without intending to be glib, this means we can experience "a bit of heaven on earth."

In the hope section of "The Character" Wesley drew on Philippians 4:6 to explain what he meant:

> *Do not worry about anything, but in everything*
> *by prayer and supplication with thanksgiving*
> *let your requests be made known to God.*

I wish Wesley had also included verse 7:

> *And the peace of God, which surpasses all understanding,*
> *will guard your hearts and your minds in Christ Jesus.*

Therein lies the key. The many and varied trials that accompany life can be rendered ineffective through prayer. According to the Apostle Paul, Christian prayer can release us from anxiety by helping us realize that God is near. Prayer can strike a balance between what is and what is to come. Sincere prayer coupled with heartfelt thanksgiving causes hope to spring up in our hearts. Thus God is glorified as our present help and future hope, and such wonderful, mysterious knowledge, "like a garrison of soldiers," will "guard" (protect) our hearts and minds, keep them safe "against the assaults of worry and fear."[7] Thus assured that God's promises are true, we can rest in hope, no matter how heavy the assault or how dreaded the trial.

"Someone to Run to"

We sat in the living room, Ruth and I, each with a cup of hot coffee, talking about hope. Ruth was saying, "When a little child is hurt, it cries out 'Mama! Mama!' and runs to her because its hope for comfort is primarily in its mother. To grow up and realize Mama is not always going to be there, that Mama cannot always make things right is a difficult experience." After pausing for a long moment, she continued, "For me, God is someone to run to." This was Wesley's conviction as well. Hope is running to God with the sure conviction that God will always be there. Hope is knowing that God will always make things right, sooner or later.

Not everyone who believes in God thinks God is always there for us. Some will tell you that God exists and in the same breath say that God is not concerned with the mundane affairs of daily life. Some people were like that in Wesley's day. They were called Deists, and many of them were intellectuals. They believed that God created the universe and then set it in motion according to its own natural laws. They taught that God sustains creation but does not intervene in any significant way in the lives of humans. For such people there is no such thing as a miracle. They believe that we cannot "run" to God with our troubles, with those pressures that threaten to overwhelm us. God is too big — too remote — too preoccupied. In effect, they believe that we must go it alone.

Deism appalled Wesley.[8] It negated hope and posed a direct challenge to the biblical view that God cares as well as creates. The Greek god Zeus may be quite happy warring and making love in his own heaven, totally unconcerned about the tragedies of life on earth, but not the God of the Hebrews, the God of Jesus Christ. What we think and how we react makes a difference to God. Wesley believed that God is concerned about even the smallest details of things that occupy us.

MAKING THINGS RIGHT

At the same time, hope in God enables us to be realistic. Life has a way of dampening many of our hopes. All too soon we learn the disappointing truth that the path is not always smooth, evil does not always seem to be punished, and everyone suffers pain at one time or another. However, Christ enables us to rethink the meaning of pain and death and to see them as temporary experiences to endure. Hope in God places other hopes in perspective. We must always remember that in Christ death itself has died. The resurrection of our Lord is the ground of our inner hope for new creation and everlasting life with God.

The early Christians were able to bear up under terrible pressures because of their anticipation of being in heaven with the Lord.

For Christians in the first century, heaven was as real as earth, if not more so. Therefore, we are urged to be patient and to bear up under unwanted troubles, realizing that such suffering has a specific goal; and that goal is not simply freedom from suffering but rather freedom for fullness of life in the kingdom of God (see 1 Peter 5:10).

For Wesley, life is never hopeless because God is "the great Physician of our souls."[9] As such, God is always aware of our pain, diagnosing our condition, and prescribing the proper "medicine" (the gospel) to cure us. Wesley's awareness of widespread human suffering led him to describe the world as "one great infirmary"; but his hope in God and in heaven also led him to work for the joy of God and the peace of heaven in this life as well. In this sense, heaven is spiritual oneness with the Almighty; it is final unity with the will of God and the joy of the Creator; it is love and it begins now.

In this way, hope in God deepens and even alters other hopes. In his sermon, "The Important Question," Wesley quoted a source to the effect that sometimes "sorrow is sweeter than joy."[10] This affirms a perspective long held in the spiritual traditions of the church; namely, that good things sometimes happen in the guise of bad things. In the midst of it all, we can be confident that God is guiding every twist and turn in our lives to bring us to heaven and to wholeness as persons. Christians can rejoice in misery as well as happiness because of the conviction that God is constantly at work reconciling all things, good and bad, to the fulfillment of God's will for us. The victory of Christian existence is seen in its most dramatic form when ordinary people are braced to rejoice in the goodness of life and to face the problems of life head-on with the God-given confidence of eternal life through our Lord Jesus Christ.

What we need is the ability to interpret what is happening to us — the good and the bad — from the standpoint of God's reconciling love. In his old age Wesley wrote the sermon "Walking by Sight and Walking by Faith."[11] Reflecting years of living with the Bible, Wesley says that neither our feelings nor our reason can take us beyond a "faint twilight" in knowing God's will. What we really need is massive doses of faith! Faith shines in our hearts and minds, bringing to light both the knowledge of God and God's design for our lives. Faith is a kind of "seeing" through the problems, opportunities, and limitations of life. Faith in turn gives birth to hope, which lifts our eyes above that which troubles us to the God who comes to help us. Hope gives us a song!

Vanish then this world of shadows,
Pass the former things away;
Lord! appear, appear to glad us
With the dawn of endless day.
O conclude this mortal story!
Throw this universe aside!
Come, eternal King of glory,
Now descend, and take thy bride.[12]

METHODISTS: A HOPEFUL PEOPLE

If we picture life and its possibilities as a young child holding a bunch of brightly colored balloons, life itself often seems to pop those balloons one by one until, by old age, only one or two faded balloons are left. If we live long enough, we will see many of our early dreams and expectations slowly vanish into the shadows. Learning to cope with the loss of hope is the subject of many self-help books. Writing about mid-life crisis, some authors propose that the best way to endure aging and maintain some balance amid the shifting circumstances of life is to diversify one's interests. Take, for example, the person who works hard to become president of the company but does not make it. Or the person who invests everything in the children, only to watch them grow up and leave home. Or one who idolizes a spouse, pouring every ounce of energy into making that spouse happy, and that person dies. To keep from crashing when our great expectations are not fulfilled, some say we should put our eggs in several different baskets. Then when a spouse dies, we can turn to other things — for example, children or career. Or when health goes, we can turn to a friend or to other interests. What we need is to diversify!

By contrast, Wesley says, "What we need is to unify!" — to place all our eggs in one basket, but in a basket strong enough to hold them. Because death and discouragement, misplaced hopes and lack of ability will take their toll, seek courage in the source of all true hope: in God who *made* us *and* who *redeems* us. Hope in God can put everything else in its proper perspective. By trusting God for our life and destiny, we can face the truth that nothing else in and of itself gives us the depth of support we need — neither spouse, nor children, nor job, nor health. Eventually all of these good things change or pass from our grasp. In God, however, we can rejoice for their place in creation; and for their and our hope of redemption.

Christian hope, therefore, brings a sense of rest. When we realize that meaningful life is not the accumulation of what we have and do but rather the gift of God, we experience peace. In addition, hope enables us to be thankful to God who loves us so freely. Life and its relationships become less competitive, and we begin to appreciate people and possessions for the realistic hopes and benefits they bring us. Hope in God keeps us from continually grasping for more, which is ultimately unsatisfying because we can never grasp quite enough. Only in God can we approximate the highest: love for God and for others, and hope in God's eternal kingdom.

For Reflection and Discussion

1. Some of the world's greatest comics have struggled with bouts of depression. Why does life seem to have this pull toward the melancholy? Or does it?

2. Jesus seemed to live with a sense of inner peace in the midst of extremely trying circumstances. What resources do you think he drew on to deal with the problems he faced?

3. As a Christian, how would you respond to others who seem to have lost all hope?

4. In what ways can the church be a sign of genuine hope in the world today?

Three

PRAYER

He was a seminary student, bright and alert, in his late twenties. As we sat and talked, I became more and more aware that he was on a serious spiritual quest, though at first it did not sound like it. "When we married," he said, "my relationship with Jeanie was almost totally a sexual one. But after five years that is changing.

"Don't get me wrong," he quickly added, "our sex life is good, but I've discovered that I now love her more deeply than ever. I can't explain it. We are becoming one, you know, like it says in the Bible" (referring to Genesis 2:23-24). Then he spoke of his relationship with God. "For a long time it has been good, though pretty much on the surface — something like my early love for Jeanie. But I know there is more . . . a deeper life . . . something closer. I want to love God as deeply as possible. I need help to do that."

This eager young man was learning an important spiritual truth about love. Love takes us where we are and plunges us deeper and deeper into itself. As such — whether physical or spiritual — love is much more than an act. True love is an intense relationship, one that is often so personal it becomes difficult to talk about. While it may be amusing to hear sexual love and divine love mentioned in the same breath, the dynamics of love, whatever the object, are in many ways the same. For my student, what had been acts of love were becoming a life of love. He wanted the same relationship with God — to move from acts of love to love itself.

I asked him what he was doing to make love grow between him and his wife. Answers poured out of him. He was doing everything he could think of to please her. They took long walks together. They spent time talking about their lives and dreams. He was sharing his life with her. As he told me this, he stopped abruptly. A light turned on in his mind. Why, it is the same with God! If he wanted to move beyond acts of love to love itself, he would need to share himself with God freely and lovingly. He needed to spend time with God, talking *and* listening.

This is what the church means by prayer, and John Wesley was

convinced that there is no better way to grow in God's love than
through prayer.

LIFTING UP OUR HEARTS

John Wesley's understanding of prayer is easy to grasp: "Prayer
is lifting up the heart to God."[1] The key word is *heart*. And what is
our heart? Used in this poetic way, *heart* refers to the vital center of
our deepest needs. I suppose we could also say it is our essential
self. For example, Jesus urges us to accumulate spiritual rather than
earthly treasures because, as he said, we set our hearts on what
we treasure most (see Matthew 6:19-21). If we "give our hearts" to
stocks and bonds, possessions and position, that is what gets all of
our attention. If we treasure God's will and kingdom, then God will
have all of us.

For Wesley, to lift one's heart in prayer was as natural for
Christians as talking with one another. As a matter of fact, prayer
is a form of talking — talking with and listening to God. Therefore,
prayer is not just a spiritual discipline or a duty to be performed.
Prayer is a relationship of confidence and intimacy. It is communi-
cating (communing) with the living God.

BECOMING PRAYER

A story is told of an Eastern Orthodox spiritual master who,
when asked by a novice about how to say prayers, answered, "Monks
do not say prayers; they become prayer." This is an apt description
of what Wesley wanted for Methodists. Wesley would have liked to
have said, "Methodists become prayer."

What does to "become prayer" mean — to pray all the time?
On this issue Wesley turned to 1 Thessalonians 5:16-18 for insight.
Bidding his readers farewell and leaving them with some last-
minute words of encouragement, the Apostle Paul wrote

> *Rejoice always, pray without ceasing,*
> *give thanks in all circumstances;*
> *for this is the will of God in Christ Jesus for you.*

Pray without ceasing. The Book of Psalms also sheds some light
here. In Psalm 1:1 and 2, we read that the righteous person prefers
God's Word to the advice of the wicked. The upright person
"meditates" on God's way "day and night." Likewise, in Psalm 119,

a collection of short prayers, the psalmist says to God, "I will meditate on your precepts, and fix my eyes on your ways" (verse 15). Again, in verse 20, "My soul is consumed with longing for your ordinances [teachings] at all times," and in verse 97, "Oh, how I love your law! It is my meditation all day long." These lines show the intensity with which one can be drawn to God. Such a person can be said to pray all the time, or at least to move in and out of prayer in a more or less unbroken way.

In the mid-seventeenth-century lived a Carmelite monk known simply as Brother Lawrence. Little is known about him except for a few letters and "conversations" which show his single-minded desire to always practice the presence of God. We have no evidence that Wesley knew of Lawrence directly, though he surely read references to him in the writings of the Roman Catholic Archbishop, François Fénelon, with whom Wesley was well acquainted. Lawrence was a cook at his monastery as well as the spiritual guide for many people. In one of his "conversations," the following was recorded as Lawrence's thought on "unbroken converse" (conversation) with God.[2] The monk advised his readers that all they needed was to be serious about the fact that God is always with them. God is our constant companion; therefore, we should treat God as exactly that, our friendly, concerned companion. This means we can speak to God at any moment, asking God's help or expressing gratitude for the good things happening around us. Thus, one can be in prayer at any time — when one is cooking dinner or singing a hymn. God is being equally honored and encountered at both times. Granted, holding such ideals might seem easier in a monastery where life appears to be a little simpler. But Wesley, like Lawrence, insisted this could be the normal experience of every Christian. An all-consuming love for God can describe a Christian at home, on the job, with friends, in trouble, at play — anywhere! This can only be true if prayer is something we *become*, not just something we *do*.

TALK WITH US, LORD!

What keeps prayer alive? It is the certainty that our petitions and praises are heard by the Lord. By "heard" I mean that our communication makes an impression on God. Jesus assures us that prayers for good things draw a response from God. Comparing God with a loving parent, Jesus says that God interacts with those who seek God by listening with compassion, acting on their behalf, and speaking back.

But how does God speak back to us? Usually through the scripture and, on occasion, through a sermon. God also communicates with us through our reflection on the created world, and through the church. I have talked with good friends who say they have heard God speak in an audible way just as I might speak to them. But regardless of the ways God chooses, for Wesley, the primary way God communicates with us is during prayer.

Fénelon wrote that, to the same extent we talk to God, God will talk to us. Therefore we ought to be silent as much as possible so that we "may listen in the stillness" of our hearts.[3] Taking a cue from Fénelon and other spiritual writers, Wesley said that though he does not know how it happens, the Holy Spirit lets us know that God is active in our lives.[4] This language of the Spirit, the voice of God, is heard inwardly by those whose hearts are sensitized to God. Just as we have ears to hear one another, Wesley taught that we have spiritual "ears" that listen to God. As far as Wesley was concerned, this inward impression of God on our spirits can be direct and beyond question.

When this happens, our hearts agree with Charles Wesley in his hymn "For Believers Rejoicing."

> *Talk with us, Lord, thyself reveal*
> *while here o'er earth we rove;*
> *Speak to our hearts, and let us feel*
> *The kindling of thy love.*
>
> *Thou callest me to seek thy face —*
> *'Tis all I wish to seek;*
> *To attend the whispers of thy grace,*
> *And hear thee inly speak.*
>
> *Let this my every hour employ,*
> *Till I thy glory see,*
> *Enter into my Master's joy,*
> *and find my heaven in thee.*[5]

As you might expect, the notion that God would indeed talk with us occasionally got the Wesleys in hot water. Such convictions sounded too much like fanaticism to suit some of their critics. Some thought those Methodists were just more in a long line of "enthusiasts" making wild claims about what God was doing or would do. Wesley countered by saying that proper prayer is shaped and informed by scripture and by church tradition. Methodists were no weird sect claiming that they alone received messages from God.

Another matter arises here. I have talked with Christians who felt they were ignored by God when their prayers were not answered the way they wanted. This can be very troubling, especially when what we pray for seems crucial to us. Wesley wrestled with this problem and solved it in terms of Romans 8:28: "We know that all things work together for good for those who love God, who are called according to his purpose." In this remarkable verse, Wesley saw something of a divine plan for the salvation of the world. God, Wesley believed, has charted out a general plan to redeem the world, and that plan involves all that concerns us individually. Though he differed from John Calvin who taught that our destinies are predetermined before birth, Wesley believed that God will use all that happens to us for our final deliverance and glory. Thus, regardless of what happens, we can trust God to work things out for our greater good, though we cannot always see that good ourselves.[6]

This means that God never ignores us and our felt needs. In fact, Jesus said that God knows our needs before we approach God with them (see Matthew 6:25-34). Our prayers are not uttered to inform God about our situation but to continually prepare our hearts to trust God's goodwill toward us and God's providential care over us.[7] We do not pray to move God in a certain direction but to move ourselves to trust God with everything. I have noticed over the years that the more mature Christians become, the fewer demands they make on God.

Our attitude should be like that of a young boxer I saw on television one Saturday afternoon. In just a few minutes he was to enter the ring for a very important fight in his aspiring career. If he won that fight he would become the number one contender for the world title in his weight class. A television interviewer tried to add some drama by reminding the boxer just how crucial this fight was to him. "Yes, it is important for me," the boxer said. "I certainly want to win if I can. But I can say that, win or lose, I praise the name of Jesus Christ."

As you can imagine, that unexpected response set the interviewer back for a moment. The boxer knew a great truth: that Christians love and serve God for who God is, not for what God gives. In the same way, we pray by faith and live by faith. The outcome of our lives is God's affair. We are confident that God will do right by us! Therefore our prayers can be peaceful, as Wesley said, full of hope and love.

THE LORD HELPS US PRAY

You may be asking, "If prayer is so natural, then why is it so diffi-cult to do?" Assuming there is no problem with disobedience in our lives, there are several possible answers to this question. First, we may think God is so exalted and we are so limited that a great distance exists between us. The gospel attempts to break down this kind of thinking. The Spirit of God is closer than our next breath. The Lord Jesus helps us by living with us and in us, breaking down spiritual and emotional barriers between ourselves and God. To be able to accept the fact that God is always near us to help us is a great relief.

Second, we may wrongly assume that "dry" periods automati-cally mean something is wrong in our relationship with God. A friend of mine remarked, "My prayer life is in a real slump. I'm not getting anywhere. I don't know what's wrong." Probably nothing was wrong. Spiritual writers consistently teach that feelings fluctu-ate. And some think it possible that occasionally the Lord may be silent so we will take speaking with God more earnestly. Every-body's saint, Francis of Assisi, was known for his intense prayers that often flooded him with the warmest feelings. Yet, in spite of his close walk with the Lord, Francis experienced long periods when God seemed to be absent. Instead of causing him to doubt the goodness of God, these times provoked Francis to more fervent prayer. God may be saying to us, "If you look closely enough and hard enough, you will find me beside you."

Third, we may pay too much attention to elaborate forms of prayer. Wesley believed that Jesus tried to help us know how to pray by giving us the Lord's Prayer. This simple prayer is found in Matthew 6:9-13. Wesley called it "a most perfect and universal form of prayer."[8]

In this prayer, Jesus told us first to begin by praising God as our heavenly parent. Second, we then express the desire that God's will be done over the whole earth just as it is done in heaven. Third, we speak our needs to God for daily necessities, for forgiveness and the strength to forgive others, and for the faith to be triumphant during trials. The fourth part, omitted in some ancient manuscripts, is a doxology praising God's power and glory. Wesley believed that by meditating on the structure of this model prayer we can develop confidence that we are praying according to God's will.

To realize that God wants to be in communion with us takes a lot of pressure off us. Unimportant is the amount of time we spend in prayer or the words or phrases we use. (Wesley knew that formal, written prayers, though beautiful, could become powerless.) The ultimate objective of all prayer is to share ourselves completely with God and thus to experience God more fully. Toward that end Wesley called his followers to walk in prayer.

METHODISTS: A PRAYING PEOPLE

In his sermon, "The Means of Grace," Wesley said that prayer is one of the chief means of grace.[9] By this he meant that prayer is one of the main ways God has chosen to draw us closer to God. For Christians, to pray is to lift our hearts to God in confidence and to recognize that we are totally dependent on the mercy and love of God. To pray is to be assured that prayer is one of the most intimate ways that God shares with us. And, if we give ourselves to prayer, we do not just pray; we become prayer. One of the exciting happenings in the Methodist revival was the renewal of prayer in the lives of zealous Christians. And one of the exciting things happening in today's church is a renewed interest in prayer.

For Reflection and Discussion

1. Authors who write about prayer often emphasize that prayer is not only speaking (or making our requests known); it is also (and just as important) listening. What is your experience with listening in prayer and why do you think this aspect of prayer is often so difficult for people?

2. What does the concept of "becoming prayer" mean to you?

3. Of the many different people you know, think of one you would want to pray for you. What is it about this person that gives you confidence in his or her prayers?

4. When we pray the prayer that Jesus taught (the Lord's Prayer), we ask God to provide for our daily needs, to forgive us as we forgive others, to keep us from evil, and to bring the life of heaven into our lives here on earth; we also praise God. What parts or dimensions of the Lord's Prayer do you think we most need to rediscover in the church today?

Four

LOVE

To be a Christian in the first century was perilous indeed. Following Jesus' crucifixion, all but one of the original disciples, not including Judas, died a martyr's death.

Minorities who are pressured by others should easily be able to empathize with the members of the early church. A monstrous situation exists when prejudiced minds stereotype groups and consider them unworthy of having even basic human rights; or worse, judge them as subhuman and unfit to live. A Jew among Nazis or an African American among the Ku Klux Klan understands better than most of us the terror of insane power and demonic values. In many ways such persecuted peoples are kin to Christians who in other ages and places have been forced to bear their witness in an atmosphere of hatred and intolerance. By the same token, Christians, of all people, should be able to understand and stand with minorities who suffer persecution.

One of John Wesley's favorite parables was that of the good Samaritan. In this teaching of Jesus, freely given love triumphs over prejudice, hatred, and rejection. Though the parable intends to show the saving love of God in Christ, it is also a reminder that true love disregards personal and social barriers in the face of human need. Wesley believed that such love is the only way we can successfully counter the evils that threaten us.

THE PATHOS OF GOD

As he lay dying, one of John Wesley's last requests was that his sermon "God's Love to Fallen Man" be "scattered abroad and given away to everyone."[1] In death as in life, Wesley wanted to proclaim by every means possible the good news of God's limitless love. Written nine years earlier, this sermon contained the central message of the Methodist movement: "We love [God] because he [God] first loved us" (1 John 4:19). Wesley's brother, Charles, captured the highlights of early Methodism's convictions about

God's great love in a hymn "describing inward religion," the second and third stanzas of which are as follows:

> *We who in Christ believe,*
> *That he for us hath died,*
> *We all his unknown peace receive,*
> *And feel his blood applied;*
> *Exults our rising soul,*
> *Disburdened of her load,*
> *And swells unutterably full*
> *of glory and of God.*
>
> *His love surpassing far*
> *The love of all beneath,*
> *We find within our hearts, and dare*
> *The pointless darts of death.*
> *Stronger than death or hell*
> *The mystic powers we prove;*
> *And conqu'rors of the world, we dwell*
> *In heaven, who dwell in love.*[2]

God's love is suffering love. We see this clearly in Charles Wesley's lines about the death of Jesus. Christ "for us hath died" and through his death has given us peace and life. "Our rising soul" has been relieved of its "load" (of guilt) and "swells unutterably full . . . of God." It is a beautiful paradox that a dying Lord unleashes "mystic powers" that are "stronger than death or hell." It was at the point of suffering that God in Christ identified most fully with us. We are frail and subject to pains of spirit and body on our way through life. We fight with everything in us against the destructive forces that threaten and erode life. It is precisely here, at the point of our struggle with hopelessness, that Christ embraces us and, drawing us to himself, fills us with joy and hope. This is the love of God in action!

The renowned Jewish scholar, Abraham Heschel, says the prophets of Israel were overcome by the pathos of God. According to Heschel, the word *pathos* means that "God is never neutral" where we are concerned.[3] God, quite literally, carries a burden for our lives, a burden that spills over into Jesus as Emmanuel (God with us). As Emmanuel, Jesus becomes involved in our hurts and fears. He is full of compassion, yearning to touch and heal our broken spirits. Today we might call Jesus' attitude one of solidarity with us.[4] And in Jesus, God assumes the same role God eventually expects of each of us — a servant role. Thus the great Creator chose the life of Jesus, poured out for helpless people in continual self-giving all the way to the cross, as the supreme way to show us what love is. This is the gospel that moved Wesley and his followers to spend themselves in selfless ministries for Christ. This was — and is — the good news!

Nowhere was the explosive love of God celebrated with more enthusiasm than among nineteenth-century frontier Methodists. This was especially evident in their campmeeting songs. Gathered in the open fields, sometimes by the thousands, rugged settlers listened to preachers such as Peter Cartwright, Lorenzo "Crazy" Dow, and others paint in vivid colors the possibilities of grace for every man, woman, and child. And filled with excitement, those Methodists sang their testimonies in the simple lyrics of frontier life.

Some of their music is still popular — the "old songs," we call them. They were usually songs of gusto, songs of grace received, songs of personal happiness. They were filled with a faith of possibility, not just for the individual but for the emerging nation. Standing on the old site of the Cane Ridge campmeeting held in 1801, just outside of Paris, Kentucky, one can still hear the faint echo of frontier men and women singing a campmeeting favorite: "Come, thou Fount of every blessing, tune my heart to sing thy grace.[5]

LOVE GETS WITH IT!

Jesus set the standard for our lives when he said, " 'You shall love the Lord your God with all your heart, and with all your soul, and with all your mind.' This is the greatest and first commandment. And a second is like it: 'You shall love your neighbor as yourself' " (Matthew 22:37-39). This twofold theme is picked up by the apostle John and used in his writings in the word *believe*: To believe in Christ means to confess him as Savior and Lord *and* to shape one's life according to his teachings.[6] If we say we believe in him, we do what he says.

The love of God released in our hearts is an active love. In his sermon "On Visiting the Sick," John Wesley tried to show exactly what this means. The biblical background for the sermon comes from Matthew 25:34-46. Speaking on our being accountable to God,

Jesus said,

> *Then the king will say to those at his right hand, "Come, you*
> *that are blessed by my Father, inherit the kingdom prepared*
> *for you from the foundation of the world; for I was hungry and*
> *you gave me food, I was thirsty and you gave me something to*
> *drink, I was a stranger and you welcomed me, I was naked*
> *and you gave me clothing, I was sick and you took care of me,*
> *I was in prison and you visited me."*

"But Lord," the upright will say, "we did not do these things for you because we never saw you in such desperate straits." Then, Jesus said, "Truly, I tell you, just as you did it to one of the least of these who are members of my family, you did it to me" (see Matthew 25:38-39). Wesley observes that for Jesus' listeners, salvation rested not only in what they believed in their hearts but also in what they did with their Godgiven love.

The instance of visiting the sick, for Wesley, represented the biblical principal that true followers of Jesus do what they can to meet the needs of others. In addition, whenever we minister to someone's troubles — emotional, physical, or relational — we are ministering to the Lord himself, for Jesus hides himself in the trying circumstances of the needy. To Wesley it did not matter whether the needy were Christian or not. The fact that the needy are human beings desperate for care qualifies them to be our neighbors. Whether a neighbor is likeable or not, a family member or a sworn enemy, does not matter. Our neighbor is anyone in need. This is a serious matter, for as Jesus continued to say according to the Matthew passage, to see someone in need and fail to help jeopardizes our standing before God!

Wesley recognized that one does not have to be a Christian to love one's family or to work for the betterment of one's community. There are basic "feelings of humanity" common to all people that foster family unity and social harmony.[7] Those feelings are the fabric of which heroes and heroines are made, especially when they sacrifice themselves for someone else. Yet Jesus Christ has a profound effect on us, regardless of how loving we may seem to be or how self-giving we are on behalf of others. Christ brings enrichment and definition to the love God gives to all of us. This is indeed a step beyond the ordinary.

DOING THE IMPOSSIBLE

On the whole, most people would rather have peace than war. Normally we do not want to fight. We prefer to bluff, with the hope that our bluff is not called.[8] We do not easily commit violence unless we are cornered, and even then we prefer flight to fight. This is also true nationally. Professional soldiers know the rest of us must be goaded into battle. In the Second World War, for example, posters were used by *all sides* to portray their enemies as vicious, monstrous predators, ready to do the vilest things to family, country, and even one's national art treasures. Nazi Germany, Italy, Ireland, France, the United States, and other nations used brightly colored posters to inflame the passion, loyalty, and fear of the common person. Nations must teach people to hate if they expect them to fight their wars.[9]

Though some enemies must be manufactured, many spring to life by themselves. Jesus told us the dreaded truth that there are enemies about, his and therefore ours, who do what they can to hinder the proclamation and living of the gospel. In the Sermon on the Mount, our Lord told the multitude,

> *Blessed are you when people revile you and persecute you and utter all kinds of evil against you falsely on my account. Rejoice and be glad for your reward is great in heaven, for in the same way they persecuted the prophets who were before you (Matthew 5:11-12).*

These enemies are bold in their sins and teach falsehood for truth.[10] Such people, the Lutheran martyr Dietrich Bonhoeffer said, are to be served.[11] They are, as Jesus states, to be the objects of our self-giving love. Though we are to treat them with caution, we are also to pray for them and do good to them, not out of fear but because we "imitate the love of God."[12] In this, Christians show plainly that the power in them is from God.

In Wesley's "Sermon on the Mount, III" he says we should take heart when our enemies turn up the heat. Why? Because

> *[God's] ear is never heavy to the threatenings of the persecutor or the cry of the persecuted. His eye is ever open and his hand stretched out to direct every [sic] the minutest circumstance. When the storm shall begin, how high it shall rise, which way it shall point its course, and when and how it shall end, are all determined by his unerring wisdom.*[13]

Wesley reminds us that Christians usually suffer "lighter" kinds of trials such as the loss of friends and strained relationships with family. On rare occasions some Christians must endure heavier trials. Wesley says all such trials are "the very badge of our discipleship" — the way in which we respond to trials is an index of God's transforming grace in our lives. We can never completely relax because the enemy of our soul prowls like a hungry lion, always on the lookout for someone to devour. But, by God's enabling grace, we can be as our Lord: doing good, facing opposition when necessary, obeying God to the end, assured we will hear God say, "Welcome, my child, into the kingdom."

BY GOD'S ENABLING GRACE

The cross is the most important symbol of the church's faith. For Roman Catholics it is a three-dimensional symbol of Christ crucified or risen; for Eastern Orthodox Christians it is a two-dimensional painting (or icon); for Protestants it is a bodiless cross, usually in the Roman or Celtic style. For every Christian, regardless of the shape of his or her faith, the cross is a stark reminder that Christ came into the world to do for us what we could not do for ourselves, namely, to free us from sin and guilt so that we could become happy, fulfilled people. The meaning of the cross is one of the three great mysteries of Christianity, the other two being the incarnation and the resurrection of Jesus. The cross speaks of the free gift of God's grace. Horrible beyond description in its actual historical use, the cross is now a sign of mercy and freedom. On it, the Gospel writer says, religious leaders tried to destroy Jesus; on it, the Hebrews writer says, Jesus destroyed the works of the evil one. (See Matthew 27:20, King James Version; Hebrews 2:14; and Colossians 2:13-15.)

In Wesley's *A Collection of Hymns for the Use of the People Called Methodist* is a short section on "Describing Formal Religion." Formal religion, the religion of Wesley's youth, was a faith that considered God's saving love as something of a final reward for a life well lived. It was a kind of moralism, a form of religion, what Wesley called "works-righteousness." Wesley saw works-righteousness as the vain attempt to earn God's favor with the expectation that God will reward such effort with eternal life. That was the kind of religion that had prompted Wesley to live a highly regimented life of devotion to God and service to others, particularly the poor. It also impelled him to spend two years as a missionary to the American Indians in Georgia. But it left him tired and depressed, joyless and frustrated.

The force with which the reality of God's free gift of righteousness through the merits of Christ alone hit Wesley is indicated in the first volume of his sermons. Sermons one and two, "Salvation by Faith" and "The Almost Christian," launch broadsides against the formal religion Wesley saw at work in the popular faith of his day. The first line of "Salvation by Faith" sets the standard for what is a constant theme in Wesley's preaching: that all of God's blessings are given to us freely.[14] Whether or not we are worthy of them is not the question. It is hard to miss his point: There are no works of any kind, either preceding or following our commitment to Christ, that in any way *earn* any merit or right standing before God. Our only claim to salvation rests on a full reliance on the blood of Christ; a firm trust in the merits of his life, death, and resurrection; a sure confidence in Christ alone; a cleaving to him as our salvation.

The anti-Methodists responded by accusing Wesley of being fanatical. They demeaned Wesley's view of Holy Communion as "magic" and considered his intense spirituality to be blatant foolishness. The "love feast," a favorite Methodist observance, was satirized in print as outright debauchery. Wesley tried to counter these accusations by appealing to scripture and tradition, but seemingly to little avail. All his life he claimed fidelity to the doctrine and order of the Church of England, defending what he believed to be its true understanding of salvation through Christ. Though criticism of Wesley diminished significantly toward the middle years of the Wesleyan awakening (1750s-1760s), in the beginning no holds were barred in the attempt to characterize the Wesleys as charlatans at best and heretics at worst.

Does all this say good works are unimportant? Not at all, Wesley would answer. Good works, which are really acts of love, are the sure signs of grace received, or at least hoped for. They are the natural, spontaneous responses of the happy heart. Christians can no more stop working than God can stop loving. In fact, we now look for ways to show love for God and God's creation because we share in God's own nature, and God is love. Good works are not a bargaining chip in our hands but the outpouring of a thankful heart.

METHODISTS: A LOVING PEOPLE

Through love Christians come to see Christ as their universal friend, God as their indulgent Parent, and every person as their neighbor. There is an intimacy, a "closing with Christ," Wesley said, that takes place as love is shared in prayer, worship, and good works. Love comes back to us when we give it away. Love is like a healthy tree bearing good fruit, in particular the fruit of humility, gentleness, and patience. Love molds Christian character, as we see in the great love chapter in the New Testament, 1 Corinthians 13:4-8a.

> *Love is patient; love is kind; love is not envious or boastful or arrogant or rude. It does not insist on its own way; it is not irritable or resentful; it does not rejoice in wrongdoing, but rejoices in the truth. It bears all things, believes all things, hopes all things, endures all things. Love never ends.*

Concluding his sermon, "On Charity," Wesley wanted everyone to be "secure" in this one point: to hold fast that "humble, gentle, patient love" given us through the merits of Christ. Only in this way will we be able to "inherit the kingdom prepared from the foundation of the world."[15]

For Reflection and Discussion

1. The parable of the good Samaritan shows that the love of God and neighbor knows no social or cultural boundaries. Where in your life or community have you experienced a love that crosses such boundaries? Where has it been most difficult to live out what Jesus' parable teaches?

2. The role of feelings in relation to love can be very confusing. Some say that the greatest love is one that is given out of a sense of duty and obedience, whether the giver feels anything or not. Others (like John Wesley) point out that love grows with a sense of being loved: "We love because God first loved us." How do you think these statements compare with Jesus' command to love God with all your heart, mind, and strength, and your neighbor as yourself?

3. Some say that the love of God is hidden in the tragedies of our lives. Do you think this is true and, if so, how would you describe this kind of love?

Five

GENTLENESS

Sooner or later, regardless of where we live or how, all of us raise our voices against our own generation. This begins in adolescence; and for some it never ends. The church itself is a perpetual adolescent in that it is at constant war with its troubled surroundings, what the biblical writer John called "the world." More often than not the church struggles with what George Santayana called a society "that talks of freedom and is a slave to riches."[1] And like the poet, we sometimes feel smothered by a system that seems to promote greed and to reward manipulative power. Much of the time we feel powerless to change things or even to redirect social energies toward service rather than production, toward human dignity rather than the desire to dominate.

The poet not only helps us diagnose our problem, but he also points us to "what is needful" to correct things. We need "a staunch heart, nobly calm." With such a disposition we will "learn to love . . . only what is eternal."[2] And this loving of the eternal — of love itself, and hope and God — will help us rise above the undertow of envy, greed, and anger that threatens us.

This sounds good, but where will we get this kind of sustaining conviction? Santayana thought that getting in touch with nature would help us reorder our priorities about what we need for our lives. But others, such as author and social critic Aldous Huxley, think our hope rests not in nature but in the power of reason. If we can sit down together and put aside our passions for a while, then there is some possibility of our being able to effect change. Education is the handmaid of peace. Without it we are doomed to continue a downward spiral into social disintegration and the dominance of the "mass mind."[3]

John Wesley was also a realist but not a pessimist. He, too, saw people looking for meaning in illusions, suckered by their egos to believe that they could rise above history and be the exception. As much as Wesley appreciated formal education, he, too, saw little hope of ultimate help in universities, politics, and science. But

30

unlike Santayana, who looked to nature for an answer, and Huxley, who searched for a saving cause, Wesley put his hope in God who alone can keep us from becoming victims of our own folly. With confidence in God's power Wesley described a Methodist as the kind of person good people really want to see.

BLESSED ARE THE GENTLE

When George Bush was running for the U.S. presidency, he said he wanted America to become a kinder, gentler nation. Whether or not he was able to help foster that spirit is up to history to decide, but we could readily identify with his vision because we had witnessed violence in our own country and even greater violence in other parts of the world. Actually, George Bush was expressing a wish as old as classical Greek literature, dating from the fourth century before Christ. The word *gentle* was used then to describe the strong king who was a kind leader, who showed particular regard for the poor. It was also a hallmark for the philosopher who stood calm in the face of insults or the judge who showed mercy in passing sentence. To be strong yet tender was valued highly. Contrary to what we might think at first, there is power in being gentle!

For the Hebrews, the idea of gentleness had a somewhat different meaning. The Old Testament portrays God's rule as one of friendliness and grace. "The Lord is merciful and gracious," the psalmist writes, "slow to anger and abounding in steadfast love" (Psalm 103:8). No one in the ancient world doubted God's might — gods were supposed to be all-powerful. But being merciful was another matter. One of the unique perspectives on God in the Old Testament is that the Lord is kind; more than that, God is a loving warrior-king who fights for God's beleaguered people. When required, divine justice can be swift and terrible; yet God's desire is that the people rest in God's love like a weaned child upon its mother's breast (see Psalm 131). A surface reading of the Old Testament may lead us to think God is often aloof, even judgmental. The truth is that God sees to the needs of God's people, even when they do not know it.

> *Yet it was I who taught*
> *Ephraim to walk,*
> *I took them up in my arms;*
> *but they did not know that I*
> *healed them.*

I led them with cords of human
kindness,
with bands of love.
I was to them like those
who lift infants to their
cheeks.
I bent down to them and fed them (Hosea 11:3-4).

The Lord bent down to feed them, the prophet says, because, exploited and destitute, they were at the mercy of their foes. Such displacement, however, was only temporary. Soon even the memory of "the wicked" will be gone and "the meek [the gentle] shall inherit the land, and delight themselves in abundant prosperity" (Psalm 37:11).

According to the Hebrew prophets, the depth of God's love would finally be seen in the Messiah. The Messiah would identify with the poor, including the spiritually poor — those whose hearts were crushed because of sin. And in the New Testament, according to Mary's song of praise in Luke 1:46-55, Jesus the Messiah defends the rights of the poor and restores their lost fortune and relatedness to God. In fact, gentleness is not only a characteristic of the Messiah's rule, it is an example for Christians to follow (2 Corinthians 10:1). Jesus' gentleness is an attitude open to God's authentic children in all their relationships in church and in the world.

In his "Sermon on the Mount, II" Wesley said that meekness or gentleness is a gift of God that helps us keep our emotions in balance, that is, keeping anger, sorrow, and fear in proper perspective.[4] Gentleness holds the reins of the Christian life, taming our passions or drives, even to channeling the more unruly ones (unnamed by Wesley) for noble purposes. This is a wonderful gift indeed! Gentleness produces kindness, contentment, and patience. In another place,[5] Wesley quotes from 1 Peter 3:8-9 in an attempt to show how important gentleness is in our relationships with others.

> *Finally, all of you, have unity of spirit, sympathy, love for one another, a tender heart, and a humble mind. Do not repay evil for evil or abuse for abuse; but, on the contrary, repay with a blessing. It is for this that you were called — that you might inherit a blessing.*

In the Sermon on the Mount, Jesus' teaching, "Blessed are the meek," carries a meaning very important for Wesley's understanding of the mission of the church. The meek, or gentle, are those people who are eager to conform to God's will.[6] They do not automatically assume that their own perspectives are right but seek to know God's will and then do it as quickly as possible. This is what Wesley seems to mean by *yieldingness*, an awkward word but one packed with implications.[7] Yieldingness, according to Wesley, is a "readiness to submit to others," in particular to those who hold the pastoral office. Such a gentle person is "easy to be convinced of what is true." To be gentle is to have an open mind, a willing mind, a submissive mind. It is not to be mind-less but to mind God and to listen to sermons and spiritual advice with a sincere desire to know the truth.

THE GENTLE AT WORK

In its chaotic history England knew some hard times when religion and politics were in conflict. The sixteenth-century historian John Foxe wrote a devastating chronicle on the martyrs of the church, focusing on those of the Roman Catholic and Protestant rift from the reign of Henry VIII to Queen Mary. With a writ of divine right in one hand and wooden stakes in the other, the crown, with the blessing of the church, used the gospel as justification for its brutal use of power. By the eighteenth-century the best Christian was a quiet Christian. When the Methodists began to show some excitement for their faith, religious interests became newsworthy again. I am convinced that had Wesley not been able to dialogue with people in high places and present Methodists in a somewhat favorable light, the movement would have been stopped by political force.

One thing was certain: the gentle people could only spread their message by means compatible with their goal, and that was to peacefully present the gospel of Jesus Christ to as many people as possible. To accomplish this, Wesley suggested four things: Preach the gospel anywhere and by any means you can; publish what is happening in books, magazines, and letters; demonstrate your faith in the societies (small confessional prayer groups); and be active in relief work for the poor. Doing this, Methodists would show their true colors, that they were a people dedicated to a simple gospel, to openness in their work, to fidelity to one another, and to helping the poorer classes (from which many Methodists came).

In a way, the early Methodist movement reminds me of the work of Mother Teresa of Calcutta. Born in Yugoslavia, she was moved by the gospel while in her mid-teens. Without much of a program but with a strong desire to serve the poor, she later left for India, where she began a ministry to those she called "the poorest of the poor." She never intended to start a religious order, but as people heard about her, they were attracted to her work. Gradually more and more people came to her, seeking ways to minister in the name of Christ. Eventually some order was needed and a "rule" was drafted by which Mother Teresa and her followers would live. Over the years the movement spread and gained influence until today, as we know, it has worldwide recognition as an outstanding charity.

Likewise the Wesleys did not intend to start anything new. All they wanted in the early days was to preach the Christ that had come to mean so much to them. Like Mother Teresa, though, the collective power of the gentle moved toward organization, an organization dedicated to the highest ideals of its founders. These are the ideals that we find in "The Character of a Methodist."

THE MIND OF CHRIST

Jesus addressed the crowds,

> *"Come to me, all you that are weary and are carrying heavy burdens, and I will give you rest. Take my yoke upon you, and learn from me; for I am gentle and humble in heart, and you will find rest for your souls. For my yoke is easy, and my burden is light" (Matthew 11:28-30).*

To many in the first century A.D. the yoke of the Mosaic Law was a heavy responsibility. Religious leaders stretched the meanings of the Law until the people reached the breaking point (see Matthew 23:4). There seemed to be a regulation for everything; freedom had turned into a nightmare. It was to such people that Jesus said his yoke was easy and his burden light. For the Lord, right standing before God was a relationship to be cultivated and enjoyed, not a list of obligations to be rigidly enforced. How necessary that is for us to hear, tired as we are of continually failing! Religious faith is not oppressive; Jesus came to show us that God is moved by the dilemmas of our lives and works to correct them. Faith is much more than a written code; it is a love relationship. This word truly makes us free!

The Apostle Paul urged people to place their hopes in such a redeemer. By growing in Christ, Paul said, we become like him. We can have his "mind" — that same way of thinking about life that

Jesus had. In Philippians 2:5-8, the Apostle tells us what the mind of Christ is like:

> *Let the same mind be in you that was in Christ Jesus,*
> *who, though he was in the form of God,*
> *did not regard equality with God*
> *as something to be exploited,*
> *but emptied himself,*
> *taking the form of a slave,*
> *being born in human likeness.*
> *And being found in human form,*
> *he humbled himself*
> *and became obedient to the point of death —*
> *even death on a cross.*

Verses 6-8 of this beautiful hymn (which extends through verse 11) speak of Christ's "humiliation," as it is often called by Bible teachers. The scenario is well known to the church. The pre-existent Christ, who "was in the form of God," did not cling tightly to his uniqueness but voluntarily took "the form of a [bond] slave," and was born "in human likeness." The one whom John calls the Word, who was "with God . . . and was God" (John 1:1), who was wrapped in divinity as in a garment, according to Paul, became a human being. This downward movement, though dramatic in itself, was not enough. The one who was a servant to others became obedient to a higher calling and lived the will of God all the way to death on the cross. Thus, the highest became the lowest! The one who was in the form (or state) of God, died a criminal's death. The mission of Jesus was therefore characterized by loving, self-giving, servant ministry and full obedience to God. This is the mind of Christ; this is the kind of mind we can have.

Philippians 2:5, Paul's admonition that we are to have the mind of Christ, was one of Wesley's favorite texts. He referred to it in almost one-third of his published sermons. The Apostle's description of Christ's incarnational life is "the greatest instance both of humiliation and obedience," Wesley said in "On Working Out Our Own Salvation."[8] In another place Wesley remarked that having the mind of Christ fills us with selfless love, makes us humble, meek, gentle to all, easy to be convinced, incredibly patient, and thankful to God.[9] As though to be sure he was not misunderstood, Wesley drew on Galatians 5:22, linking the mind of Christ with the fruit of the Spirit; God filling us with love (first and foremost), joy, peace, patience, gentleness, goodness, faithfulness, and moderation.[10]

Think of it! The mind of Christ — his values, his attitudes on life, on people, on divine reality — becoming our mind! Think what it would mean if we were enabled to have Christ's perspective on ourselves and on others. We would no longer feel that we needed to control others. We would want to meet the needs of others. And best of all, we would love the will of God, following that will wherever it took us, regardless of the cost.

Charles Wesley wrote a thirteen-stanza hymn based on Philippians 2:5.[11] It is a prayer for the mind of Christ. The hymn begins with a confession.

> *O how wavering is my mind,*
> *Tossed about with every wind!*
> *O how quickly doth my heart*
> *From the living God depart!*

Then Wesley prayed that he might "feel" (know) the nearness of God, that he might behold God and know God at work in the depths of his own heart. Following this confession is a series of specific requests, each of which ends with a description of the mind of Christ. The first two stanzas show the pattern:

> *Plant, and root and fix in me*
> *All the mind that was in thee;*
> *Settled peace I then shall find —*
> *Jesu's is a quiet mind.*

> *Anger I no more shall feel,*
> *Always even, always still;*
> *Meekly on my God inclined —*
> *Jesu's is a gentle mind.*

The remaining stanzas round out the picture: Jesus' mind is also patient, noble, spotless, loving, thankful, constant, and perfect. We need to keep in mind that the way for Jesus was not always peaceful and untroubled. Events sometimes disturbed him, temptations pulled at him, and death threatened him. Yet he never wavered from gentleness toward those in need or from full obedience to God, regardless of the situation. Wesley's description of Jesus strikes a responsive chord in our hearts. Can we really have that mind? Though it may take a lifetime to fully realize, Wesley thought we could. The mind of Christ is God's gift to every sincere believer.

METHODISTS: A GENTLE PEOPLE

To believe that people can really live together in peace and mutual respect seems increasingly difficult in our time. The more philosophical among us tend to think *homo sapiens* is basically *homo furiens* and that we are doomed to live out our short existence in dog-eat-dog competition, if not in outright violence.

Even the church seems at times unable to foster among its members the high ideals to which it is committed in theory. But however far Methodists have missed the mark of authentic discipleship, they have historically given themselves to its pursuit. Indeed, by whatever label they are called, Christians have been drawn to such high ethical standards precisely because they firmly believe that this is what God intends them to be. Methodists affirm that, through grace, great changes in personal attitudes and behavior are possible — indeed, are to be expected. Human beings can in some significant way become the kinds of people the world desperately needs, not by their own strength or ability, but by the grace and power of God. And Methodists know we are in this together. We need one another, to be committed to one another and to the Christ in each of us. This is in part what it means to be a gentle Methodist.

For Reflection and Discussion

1. Some people fear that any talk of being gentle is a sign of weakness. In what ways is the life of Jesus a response to such fears?

2. Therapists have shown that "touch therapy" is an important healing agent — such as the gentle rubbing of the bodies of crack cocaine babies. In what other ways can gentleness be healing for us?

3. The biblical story portrays a God of steadfast love who draws us rather than drives us to wholeness and peace. Why doesn't sheer force work in spreading the good news of Jesus Christ?

4. Is there a point in personal or social relationships where Christians are no longer bound by the call to peace and gentleness? Explain your response.

Six

SINCERITY

"The road to hell is paved with good intentions" is an aphorism I have known from my youth. Even in childhood it required little interpretation. This saying reinforced an instinctive feeling that being sincere about something did not always mean it was right. It warned me that I had to make choices in life and that all choices did not end well. As an assistant to the pastor in Houston, Texas, I saw this tension at work in Betsy. In her mid-teens, Betsy was unattractive in dress and mannerisms, and she was the product of a shattered home. She merely wanted what every teenager wants: security, attention, acceptance. She received none of this at home, and the little she got from the church youth group was not enough to satisfy her desperation. Thinking she might be loved if she gave sex away freely, one weekend she went on a binge. Caught in a motel she was charged with prostitution. The police report logged sixteen counts against her over a three-day period. As a result of that weekend she became pregnant and her mother threw her out of the house. Though we tried every way we could to help Betsy, her life had become a living hell. There was a fatal innocence in her desire for love. She was sincere in her efforts — but sincerely wrong.

Misplaced sincerity is not always this tragic, but it always leads to a dead end. This is one reason the scriptures are filled with cautions about choosing well, about giving oneself to what will prove true and good. For example, the first psalm sets the tone for the whole psalter by putting its reader at a crossroad. One fork leads to the company of the wicked, the sinner, and the scoffer. The other fork leads to the covenant of the living God. The first leads to terrible advice, serious mistakes, and eventual destruction. The second leads to personal fulfillment, inner peace, and productivity. "Choose well," we hear the psalmist say, "because the stakes are high!" Ironically, temptations regarding love and acceptance are generally the same for the corporate executive, the homemaker, and the janitor as they were for Betsy. There are no shortcuts to a meaningful life. Sincerity must be concerned first and foremost with truth as it is, not with truth as we would like it to be. Sincerity placed in untruth is a catastrophe; sincerity placed in truth is salvation.

John Wesley believed that Methodists were on the right track because they placed all their hopes for truth in him who is the Truth (see John 14:6). Furthermore, Methodists not only want to love God with all their hearts; they design their lives to reach that goal.[1] Such sincerity is seen in Christ's prayer in the garden shortly before his arrest: "My Father, if it is possible, let this cup pass from me; yet not what I want but what you want" (Matthew 26:39). Because Jesus had a "single eye" to God's glory, the will of God became "light" to Jesus — it showed him the unmistakable way to go and gave him the assurance that God was with him all the way. The hope of the church is that Jesus' experience will become our experience.

LIVING OUR BAPTISM

One evening a Pharisee named Nicodemus came to see Jesus. His was not a social call. Nicodemus was aware of Jesus' reputation as a miracle worker. Perhaps he was present when Jesus overturned the tables of the moneychangers and sellers of sacrificial animals in the Temple, complaining they were turning God's house of prayer into a den of thieves. Nicodemus had to know more about this man. So that night Nicodemus probed Jesus about his authority and his teachings. The Lord responded by saying that Nicodemus would have to be spiritually reborn ("from above"), if he was to understand what Jesus was doing and saying. From this brief conversation we derive one of Jesus' main teachings: God's gracious love can make people new (see John 3:1-3).

This marvelous message was central to John Wesley's evangelical revival in England. Later, in America the same theme would become the main focus of frontier preaching.[2] But what exactly are the changes the living Christ produces in us? In his sermon on "The New Birth" Wesley tells us that a new Christian

1. Inwardly senses God at work in his or her heart,
2. Experiences real peace and joy,
3. Is able to begin distinguishing between good and evil,
4. Begins to grow daily in the knowledge of God,
5. Finds real meaning in prayer and praise, and
6. Desires to love all people.[3]

All of this together is what Wesley called the "great change" that God makes in our hearts. According to this, we can see that for anyone who finds God it is a new day!

Baptism represents the beginning of the Christian life. It is a formal occasion when we make vows — either for ourselves, or on behalf of our children — that we will turn our backs on evil and turn our faces toward God. Baptism is a time when we accept the conditions of the new covenant in Christ and the way God is working in our lives, which means we will walk in the ways of the Lord all our days. At baptism we are all, spiritually speaking, immature Christians. From this point on we grow toward maturity in faith in our relationships with God and with other people. The act of baptism will always remain a point of reference for our growing life of faith, for baptism is, as Wesley says, a "precious means" of God's grace.[4]

It has been said of the great reformer Martin Luther that, when he felt tempted beyond what he thought he could bear he cried out, "I am baptized! I am baptized!" That reminded him that he belonged to Christ; thus he gained strength to resist the temptations he faced. Christians show sincerity when they try to live in the light of their baptismal vows. Methodists find it helpful periodically to review what they have promised at their baptism and to rededicate themselves again to God.

The sincerity of a Methodist is reflected in this Wesley prayer hymn. It remains a good standard to follow.

> *Be it my only wisdom here,*
> *To serve the Lord with filial fear,*
> *With loving gratitude;*
> *Superior sense may I display*
> *By shunning every evil way,*
> *And walking in the good.*
>
> *O may I still from sin depart;*
> *A wise and understanding heart,*
> *Jesus, to me be given!*
> *And let me through thy Spirit know*
> *To glorify my God below,*
> *And find my way to heaven.*[5]

A WISE AND UNDERSTANDING HEART

Wesley's prayer for "a wise and understanding heart" is absolutely essential if we are to "run the race" God sets before us (Hebrews 12:1). Once committed to the Christian life, we need to know how to stay in it! All around us are unfortunate examples of good and well-meaning people who started their Christian lives with enthusiasm, only to fizzle out later. Not all who begin the race cross the finish line. How can we be sure our sincerity is rightly placed? How can we make our way around the pitfalls at every turn? Wesley offered three pieces of advice that, if heeded, will serve us well.

1. *Check your progress daily*. Wesley repeatedly urged his followers to follow the Apostle Paul's advice: "Examine yourselves to see whether you are living in the faith. Test yourselves" (2 Corinthians 13:5). This is a gentle warning that, unless we are careful, we may drift away from the moorings of vital faith and, in the words of the Hebrews' writer, become "shipwrecked." The issue is whether or not we truly know Jesus in our hearts, whether he is in our lives by our loving consent and earnest desire, and whether he is actively helping us live victoriously. Wesley said we can know for a fact that Christ lives within because the Holy Spirit impresses on our hearts the reality of Christ in us.[6] Watching for signs of the life of love, joy, peace, patience — what Paul calls the fruit of the Spirit — is another powerful evidence that we are spiritually alive.

2. *Be careful what you want*. Wesley believed that all of us are born with a flaw in our character. He called it original sin. We are created in the image of God, but we have taken a different direction.[7] Left to ourselves, Wesley believed, we will wander away from God. Seen another way, this original sin is a kind of resistance, like that often seen between a small child and its parents. The same resistance echoes in the biblical story of Adam and Eve. Living in a beautiful garden, the couple enjoyed many freedoms. But there was one prohibition: they were not free to eat from the tree of the knowledge of good and evil. You know the story. Instead of loving God and enjoying their many freedoms, the pair disobeyed the one prohibition. They thought they understood their needs better than God. They paid a high price for their decision. Wesley believed that we too face much the same temptation: the temptation to take control and do what we want, even if it conflicts with what God wants for us.

The lesson is this: Check your motives before making up your mind. You may want something that will hurt you, even though it does not look that way at the moment. We can trick ourselves! We sometimes justify wrong decisions by making them appear to be the right ones. So Wesley said, "Deny yourself!" — which means, do not place your own desires above God's will for you. Positively speaking, Wesley would say, always and in everything, do only the will of God as it is shown to you. This is the only safe way to travel the road of the Christian life. Our Creator and Sustainer knows what is best for us and, because God is love, will lead us in the best way possible. God is for us!

3. **Always do the will of God.** The will of God, Wesley wrote, is nothing other than "God himself."[8] We know God is love, therefore to love is automatically God's will for us. When Jesus tells us to love God with all our heart and our neighbor as ourself, he is saying, in effect, "Let love fill you just as love fills God" (see Matthew 22:34-40). Likewise, we know God is patient; therefore we are to be patient with others. We know God is self-giving, therefore we should give our lives and labors to help others (even those who do not appreciate it!). Every aspect of God's will for us focuses on one supreme objective — that we should in all our attitudes and actions be dedicated to God alone.[9] This is the highest and the best. The will of God is our sanctification, Paul says, which means God wants our hearts to be filled to the brim with God's own life. This is what all sincere Christians want: to be conformed in every possible way to the Lord Jesus.

Sometimes the will of God is not as clear as we would like. Occasionally divinity students will say to me, "I know I am called by the Lord to be a minister, but I don't know if that means being a pastor, missionary, teacher, or something else. How can I know the specific will of God for me?" Or a businesswoman might ask, "Is it God's will for me to expand my business into another state?" A college student may wonder, "Does God want me to major in pre-med or English literature?" A couple talks with each other, "Should we buy this house or the other one? What does God want?" The underlying assumption of these questions is that God is interested in the details of our lives and wants to help us as we make important decisions. Wesley certainly believed this to be true.

But Wesley thought we sometimes ask the wrong question. Instead of, "What is God's will?" we should ask, "Of the options I have, which one will make me a more effective Christian?" Wesley suggested four ways to answer the question. First, look to see if the Bible sheds any light on our concern. After all, we may receive clear guidance from scripture. If so, we have our answer before us. If the scripture is not clear, we have a second option: Draw on experience. Based on what you know, what do you think you should do? Third, apply a little logic. If you go this way instead of that, what is likely to happen? Finally, pray for the Holy Spirit to guide you. This is not a "try this if everything else fails" approach. It indicates that we should wait for the Lord's guidance. This requires much patience, but the Spirit is our teacher and brings things to mind we had not considered before. At any rate, if these four working principles to knowing God's will are applied, Wesley believed one would know it. God will not fail us.

An Undivided Heart

In the New Testament the notion of sincerity is linked with two word groups, one of which means pure and holy, and the other, single and simple.[10] To trace each of these meanings would be valuable in itself. Yet when taken together we get the idea that sincerity conveys a genuineness, a being "up front" (not having a hidden agenda), pursuing a single aim, having unblemished sincerity. To be sincere is to live with an uncomplicated simplicity, a sort of personal wholeness or spiritual integration. As a result, we can have peace with God, even with ourselves, and, as much as possible, with other people. (I say "as much as possible" because no one can guarantee how our love will be received.) Whatever the case, this peace is not diminished by our circumstances, since it is not so much a feeling as it is a relationship, an understanding between ourselves and God. For Wesley, all of this showed that the depth of sincerity is the kind of love Jesus talked about when he said in Matthew 5:48: "Be perfect, therefore, as your heavenly Father is perfect."

This concept is difficult to talk about, since this kind of love defies definition. One can only describe instances of it. The word *perfect* does not help us much today since our use of the word is so narrow. It is almost impossible for Westerners to speak of perfection (in religious terms), clouded as it is with images of a spirituality untouchable by humans. Even Wesley's broad statement that perfection, according to scripture, is "pure love filling the heart and governing all the words and actions" is not especially helpful.[11] We live in a time when things "pure" are more of a fantasy than a possibility. Even so, the idea that a love-filled heart is perfect consumed Wesley's attention all of his adult life. One has to admire his tenacity, although he probably stirred up more controversy on this subject than anything else. We can look at it something like this: God's love can be so real in us that we become whole persons; or, God's love makes us completely happy by integrating our lives. That is saying a lot!

If this is true, and Methodists believe it is, then God's love enables us to do the unusual, that which is not a matter of course.[12] For example, the love of God in us enables us to love or value other people with the same love or value God has for them. It would certainly be *unusual*, to use Wesley's term, for people to want for their enemies the same wonderful life they want for their children or as much success for their competitors as for themselves. Yet this is what Jesus taught. When we follow through on this, we give evidence of our sincere intention to be truly Christian. As Thomas Merton, a spiritual writer, put it, to be perfect as a Christian is "in every sense a way of love, of gratitude, of trust in God."[13]

METHODISTS: A SINCERE PEOPLE

We can be sure the degree of our sincerity in both human and divine relationships will be tested. I know two men who faced similar tragedies. These men did not know each other. Both were married to women who were horribly disfigured in automobile accidents. Both couples had been married a relatively short time. Both had taken basically the same marriage vows to love their wives "for better or for worse, in sickness and in health." On their wedding day, that was an easy promise to make. Now both were shaken to the roots by what had happened. One of the men embraced his hurting wife and cared for her. The other divorced his wife, saying he could not handle what had happened. While not all tests are so dramatic, we can be sure that our sincerity will be tested too.

The Gospel writer Luke relates the following story about spiritual sincerity.

> *As they were going along the road, someone said to him [Jesus], "I will follow you wherever you go." And Jesus said to him, "Foxes have holes, and birds of the air have nests; but the Son of Man has nowhere to lay his head" (Luke 9:57-58).*

In this story a Jewish man tells Jesus he wants to be his disciple. But Jesus, seeing that the man is more interested in being known as a disciple of Jesus than really being one, tells him that there are no special privileges attached to following the Lord. In fact, he will be in need often and the going will be rough. The story ends there. We do not know what the man's response was, although from other information we have in the Gospels, we can assume he turned away from Christ and melted back into the crowd. This example shows that a person — any man or woman — may say one thing but mean something else. Sincerity comes from deep within, and it takes time to show itself.

Wesley said that "in a Christian believer love sits upon the throne . . . fills the whole heart, and reigns without a rival."[14] This is real sincerity! Love alone fires Christian zeal. Love alone embraces a broken spouse. Love alone follows Jesus when there are no immediate rewards. Love enables us to carry through with our commitments, especially when it seems impossible. Such are the gifts of God, enabling us to pursue uprightness, fidelity, and truth.

For Reflection and Discussion

1. Spiritual writers often caution us about looking to our feelings as a test of our sincerity. Why should we be cautious about our feelings?

2. The will of God revealed in the life of Jesus has always been a challenge to the way of life espoused in society. What are some of the main ways you experience conflict between what society bids and what Jesus calls you to be and do?

3. Some say that the rite of baptism has become all too easy and, hence, almost meaningless to people in many places and denominations. What would it take in your congregation for people to experience the sacrament of baptism in a richer and more meaningful way?

Seven

OBEDIENCE

The first Methodists soon became the target of political cartoons in the local news. In the eighteenth century, satire was one of the more popular ways to deal with difficult movements or ideas. (It still is — just listen to the late night talk shows!) Clearly John Wesley had a problem on his hands. He needed to let others know that Methodists had no axe to grind, just love to give. In "The Character," as we have seen already, Wesley tried to show that Methodists were not a special interest group whose intent was to irritate the government. They were not a new religious denomination or some weird cult, or a private club with a secret handshake. The only requirement for becoming a Methodist was to be serious about being upright before God. These Methodists did not want to start anything new; they simply wanted to touch base with their religious roots and recapture the thrill of being Christian.

It became very important for Wesley to show that Methodist loyalty was to the God of scripture, the one revealed in and through Jesus Christ. Methodists were not trying to rearrange church polity or doctrine, at least not at first. They wanted to keep to the Christian basics as found in the great creeds of the church and in the Thirty-Nine Articles of Religion of the Church of England to which most of them belonged. Notwithstanding his efforts to set the record straight, Methodists were still regarded by many as nothing but troublemakers. Wesley himself often received verbal abuse and, on more than one occasion, was the target for overzealous bullies with a handful of rocks. Once an angry bull was turned loose in a crowd gathered to hear Wesley preach. The group scattered and Wesley preached on. Undaunted by accusations and threats, Wesley hoped Methodists would, by word and example, demonstrate that they were friends, not enemies.

In Wesley's mind, loyalty established veracity, especially when loyalty was to biblical faith. And veracity inspires zeal, the kind of zeal that makes us want to be good and do good. In a word, Christian obedience is as natural for followers of the Lord as is breathing.

HEARING AND OBEYING

One day Jesus was in a deep discussion with some religious leaders. As this was happening, a scribe quietly observed the give-and-take. Impressed with Jesus' calm and reasoned approach, the scribe decided to ask a question himself. Addressing the Lord, the scribe asked, "Which commandment is the first of all?" (Mark 12:28). Jesus responded to the question by quoting the great *Shema*, an ancient Hebrew creed, one very familiar to the scribe. The *Shema* begins with an exhortation to ponder carefully what is being affirmed in this brief creed.

> *Hear, O Israel: the Lord our God, the Lord is one; you shall love the Lord your God with all your heart, and with all your soul, and with all your mind, and with all your strength (Mark 12:29-30).*

In the book of Deuteronomy the *Shema* is followed by instructions to "keep these words. . . . Recite them to your children," discuss them in your home, make them a sign on your person and on your house (Deuteronomy 4:6-9). The scribe would have been pleased to hear this. Then Jesus added a second commandment from Leviticus 19:18 on loving one's neighbor. For the faithful, the *Shema* was a daily reminder to love God with every fiber of one's being. The call to hear ("Hear, O Israel") was at the same time a call to obey, for in biblical language *hearing* and *obeying* come from the same root word. What was the great commandment? To love God and neighbor — that is, to love them in word *and* deed in obedience to the will of God.

As we know from reading the Old and New Testaments, not everyone who heard the words of the Lord obeyed them. Simply because the good news is announced does not mean people take it in and live by it. Quite the contrary, very often the gospel hits a wall of resistance. Actually, each of us seems to have a tension in us about relating to authority. Sometimes we want to obey, and sometimes we want to rebel.

Psychologist Gerald May says that two contradictory attitudes seem to dominate our lives. May calls these two attitudes willfulness and willingness.[1] To be willful is to be self-assertive, always calling the shots (or wanting to). Willfulness is laced with arrogance and tends to shut out opinions that differ from its own. Willingness is the opposite. Willingness means to be open to others, self-restrained, desiring to listen and wanting to learn or adjust. For May, Christian life is the graced attempt to move from willfulness to willingness in our relationship with God. Understood this way, Christian obedience is a reverential listening to God's voice, however it comes, coupled with a strong desire to live according to what one hears. Obedience is *being* first, then *doing*.

The spirit of true obedience is reflected in the Lord's Prayer at the place where Jesus says,

> *"Your kingdom come.*
> *Your will be done,*
> *on earth as it is in heaven" (Matthew 6:10).*

Commenting on this petition, Wesley wrote that Christians want to please God on earth in the same ways the angels please God in heaven.[2] This means we will pray to obey God's will *lovingly*, *willingly*, and *continually*. If we grasp what Wesley is saying, we will understand better what May means by willingness.

First, Christians want the will of God to be done on earth lovingly. Christian obedience always works for what is good, noble, and kind. Love creates an atmosphere of acceptance and patience, an atmosphere in which maximum growth can take place. From a Christian standpoint, sharing such love is actually sharing God, for God is love. Even divine justice must be understood in relation to divine love. Love does not allow wrongs to go unchallenged. And love is the graced ability to be for the other person what that person needs most: full sympathy and understanding. Such is the love of God! Like the angels of God, we are to be messengers of God's gracious love, a love that defends, protects, and cares.[3]

Second, Wesley said that we should want the will of God to be done willingly. This means we want to do God's will, whatever it is, because we prize it. One of my colleagues says we give God "permission" to work in our lives, knowing that God's "work" is what we need. Sometimes we give permission grudgingly, as if to say "O.K., go ahead and operate." But when sheer love comes into our lives, we open ourselves to it with all our hearts. Then, to use a metaphor of Wesley's, we "run" to do God's will.

Third, Wesley believed that Christians want to do God's will continually. This is a constant desire, with no stopping point. Wesley's analogy of a fruit-bearing tree is a good one here. Farmers who grow fruit know the joy of seeing a good, insect-free crop year after year. Healthy, well-kept trees continually produce good fruit.

So it is in our lives with God. The will of God, focused as it is on meeting our needs, never stops healing and helping us. And we react to grace in the same way; we too want to do God's will continually. We want, so to speak, to bear good fruit all the time. Desire meets desire! It simply never stops.

This is May's willingness in Wesley's understanding of Christian life. We open ourselves to God, desiring to know more of the Lord, wanting to do whatever pleases God, and running to help others eat from the same tree.

A Covenant of Obedience

We do not, however, fall into faith accidentally. Christian faith is the result of a human being responding favorably to the call of God. Christian faith begins with the self-revelation of God and the disclosure of the divine will. From a biblical standpoint, God breaks into the human scene; God acts. Then God calls, and the call is not a vague feeling; the call is to a commitment to the covenant. The covenant of God requires total self-dedication to its conditions. Old Testament scholar Walther Eichrodt shows us the seriousness of entering into covenant with the living God. Eichrodt comments, "The decisive requirement for admission [to the covenant] is not natural kinship but readiness to submit oneself to the will of the divine Lord of the Covenant and to vow oneself to this particular God."[4] Or, as the familiar aphorism puts it, "God has no grandchildren, only children." Everything is on a first-generation level!

Wesley developed a special service for "Such as Would Make Their Covenant with God."[5] Since it is no small thing to give oneself to God, Wesley believed a liturgy of renewal was in order, a liturgy that (1) set the conditions of the covenant, (2) called for the adoration of God, (3) gave thanksgiving for God's abundant grace, and (4) made solemn confession. Wesley's covenant service is a service of making vows to the ideals of the gospel of Christ. It is designed to help both clergy and laity reflect on what it means to deny oneself and to faithfully follow Christ, or as Wesley says, to "take the yoke of Christ upon us." Participation in this service is always a sobering experience. The high point of the liturgy is the prayer of renunciation, a prayer of humble obedience (see following page):

Minister:

O Lord God, Holy Father, who has called us through Christ to be partakers of this gracious Covenant, we take upon ourselves with joy the yoke of obedience, and engage ourselves, for love of you, to seek and to do your perfect will. And as you have shown us in him who is the Way, the Truth, and the Life, we will follow our Lord whithersoever he goes. We are no longer our own, but yours.

People:

I am no longer my own, but yours. Put me to what you will, rank me with whom you will; put me to doing, put me to suffering; let me be employed for you or laid aside for you, exalted for you or brought low for you; let me be full, let me be empty; let me have all things, let me have nothing; I freely and heartily yield all things to your pleasure and disposal.

This prayer expresses the heart of the Christian life: No matter which road we are called to travel in fulfilling God's will, Christ will be there to make it the right road. All we have to do is to be obedient to our covenant with God. This means I no longer reserve any part of my life selfishly; that I literally give everything over to God's care and use. How can we do this? It is only possible through humility and through obedience. And what will happen to us? Well, that is entirely up to God's providence. In this light the abrupt ending of the prayer is appropriate: ". . . you are mine and I am yours. So be it."

We need this Wesley covenant service to help us keep our priorities straight. We are not to aspire to places of prominence but to places of service. We are not to seek recognition for ourselves but to give recognition to others. We are not to hoard material goods but to share them. We are to consider our physical life a gift to God and then do what we can when we can and leave the rest to God. If God chooses, for whatever reasons, to put us in high places, that will be fine with us. Likewise, if God chooses the lowest places for us, that will be fine, too. The only concern we have is obedience to the God we love. To be honest, reflecting on this prayer leaves me drained, challenging as it does all my pretensions and all my aspirations.

Mix Our Friendly Souls

Christian obedience is not limited to our individual experiences of God. In biblical writings one finds a strong balance between the individual and the community of faith. Somewhat paradoxically, our destiny reflects both our personal relationship with God *and* our involvement in the company of "the called-out ones," the church.

John Wesley realized that authentic faith does not flourish in isolation.[6] Christianity is, he wrote, "a social religion." It is not a matter of "my experience" or "my church." It is "our experience" and "our church." God created us as family units and the church is the greatest family unit around! Thus, Wesley said that the church cannot exist as a group of isolated individuals; it is a body with many members.

Wesley was unashamedly "high church"; that is, he loved the church's creeds and liturgy. But Wesley did not demean other traditions. He believed all churches shared a common call to be communities set apart to worship God, to cultivate a Christian life-style, to encourage the depressed and persecuted, to be a witnessing congregation, and to confront the powers of evil. After all, we are all one in Christ, no matter what our denominational label or form of worship. Like Wesley, Methodists do not require others to hold our peculiar opinions or embrace our distinctive liturgies. We ask no more than the early church: Keep the faith God has given, love one another, and live honorably and compassionately in the world.[7]

In one of his poems, Charles Wesley emphasized that shared obedience is one of the primary supports of the Christian community. In one hymn we find the following dialog with God.

Thou God of truth and love,
We seek thy perfect way,
Ready thy choice t'approve,
Thy providence to obey,
Enter into thy wise design,
And sweetly lose our will in thine.

Why hast thou cast our lot
In the same age and place?
And why together brought
To see each other's face,
To join with softest sympathy,
And mix our friendly souls in thee?

Didst thou not make us one,
That we might one remain,
Together travel on,
And bear each other's pain.
Till all thy utmost goodness prove,
And rise renewed in perfect love.[8]

The first stanza emphasizes the communal nature of Christian obedience; together we seek God's perfect way and willingly give up our own desires in favor of doing God's will. The second stanza raises the question of why God has called us to be part of this particular community of seekers. Then the third stanza answers the question by saying we move together, by mutually sharing love and obedience to God, in order to be able to encourage one another and together to become complete in love. Again we see this clear emphasis: We are a people! So obedience leads to love, love for God and for one another. Here is a common faith, a common God, and a common goal.

METHODISTS: AN OBEDIENT PEOPLE

The abuse of authority at all levels has led many to be suspicious of words such as *obedience*, *submission*, and *loyalty*. Who in good conscience can obey the dictates of an evil government, an abusive parent, or a power-hungry church official? Does not power corrupt and absolute power corrupt absolutely, as we have heard? The Christian community has struggled with these kinds of issues for a long time, and answers are not easy to come by.

In some way each of us can share the agony of the secondary school teacher who was working toward an advanced degree in one of my classes in southern California. The class was on "Church and Society" and was going fairly well. This woman was a cheerful person, very bright and eager to be involved in class discussion. But during one session, as the function of the church was being discussed, she exploded.

"The church!" she blurted out. "All it does is preach how guilty we are." Then with voice rising and face turning red, she sputtered, "And then it charges us money to tell us how to get rid of the sins it says we have committed!" By now she was on the brink of tears. The rest of the group was silent. Slowly I tried to calm her and little by little help her distinguish between the church as it was intended to be and the church as it sometimes becomes. It was a difficult moment. She was beyond the point of rational thinking, so we took a break while she regained her composure.

In some way unknown to the rest of us, this woman had been victimized by an abusive situation. But consider what she might have said had her experience been like those of the early Christians (see Acts 2:43-47). In their midst she would have felt support, empathy, security, and graciousness. She would have been part of a people who shared what they had, who spent time together, and who loved freely from glad and generous hearts. Then obedience would have come easily, and submission would have been rewarding. Her trust would have been returned with confidence, and she would have been honored as one who bore the image of God. Wesley's life-long dream was to be part of such a people. This continues to be the dream of his followers.

For Reflection and Discussion

1. In the history of the church, the will of God has been interpreted in two basic ways: 1) as a set of detailed instructions a person can discover and follow in every circumstance (for example, what job to take, where to live), and 2) as a way of life centered in love and patterned on the life of Christ that applies in every circumstance, even when detailed instructions are not clear. How do these different views help you in thinking about the will of God and the meaning of obedience for your life?

2. John Wesley's Covenant Prayer suggests that we only discover the true benefit and joy of being a Christian when we enter the way of costly discipleship. In what ways would you say that your discipleship has been costly? What have been the benefits of accepting these costs?

3. How would you explain the importance of community — of shared corporate life — to a person who wants to try to be a Christian but insists on going it alone and avoiding other people?

Eight

GROWTH

Christians are the most optimistic people on the face of the earth. We honestly believe people's lives — and the societies they build — can be changed for the better by the power of the gospel. This view would not have been debatable in ancient times, but it is frankly incredible in a Western society that has replaced God with technology. The major problem, however, is that technology has not radically improved the general condition of the human family. In spite of our fantastic advances, we are not getting better and better every day and in every way as was forecast at the turn of the twentieth century. Instead, nations have been plunged into frightful concerns over pollution, shrinking natural resources, and the ever-present threat of nuclear holocaust, whether by an atomic bomb or by emissions from a nuclear power plant. Such massive problems are in part the result of technology. And who are the modern-day prophets rising up to warn us of what could happen if things do not change? The Christian revivalists? No, rather our prophets are scientists and naturalists!

Respected social theorist Earnest Becker believes the crux of our modern dilemma is not just in what we make but in who we are. He thinks our warlike tendencies and destructive inventions are only symptomatic of a far deeper crisis of identity. In his Pulitzer Prize-winning book *The Denial of Death*, Becker says our problems stem from the "terrifying paradox of the human condition," that we are the only animal fated to live with the frightening knowledge that life is ultimately meaningless; in the final analysis, all our heroic efforts die with us.[1]

From the standpoint of a naturalist, Becker's overall analysis of what it means to be human is often brilliant. He sheds light on many of the neuroses we suffer and on the reasons for our basic uneasiness about life. However, notwithstanding its finality, life is still important for Becker. It does take a certain heroism not to cave in, with our knowledge of the end. What keeps us from going absolutely berserk, from Becker's perspective, is our ability to craft wonderful schemes

54

of denial. In his magnificent sequel, *Escape from Evil,* Becker traces our tangled social ills to our attempts to overcome the dread of insignificance. Even so, what have we to hope for? What are we to do about what is happening to us? Perhaps post-Freudian thought, Becker speculates, "will introduce just that minute measure of reason to balance destruction."[2] Is the last word then the "minute measure" of some bit of insight to "balance destruction"? Is it true we grow old only to die, our existence an essentially meaningless blip in time?

Wesley, indeed the whole Christian tradition, shouts a resounding "No!" Here Christians find themselves at loggerheads with many elements of contemporary intellectual society. And nowhere is the line of demarcation clearer than between thinkers such as Becker and Wesley. According to Becker, we are born to die. According to Wesley, we are born to live. People grow old, all right, but not just to become frustrated older adults, filled with more fear than ever. Rather, by the grace of God centered in the resurrection of Jesus Christ, we may grow and grow and grow — forever! But the meaning we seek does not come cheaply, easily, or naturally. To paraphrase the psalmist (Psalm 20:7),

> *Some put their trust in military might and industry,*
> *but we will call upon the name of the Lord our God.*

A Pilgrim People

There are many biblical metaphors describing what being a Christian means. Living with God is variously described as

> *running a race,*
> *fighting a war,*
> *winning a boxing match,*
> *growing from infancy to adulthood,*
> *learning like an eager student,*
> *and growing love between a woman and a man.*

But perhaps the most compelling way of looking at spiritual growth is from the standpoint of taking a journey — a pilgrimage through life leading to the kingdom of God.

Usually the idea of spiritual life as a journey is taken from the account of Abram, later known as Abraham, the father of the faithful (see Genesis 12). Abram is called by God to leave his home in Ur and to go to a country unknown to him. We are not told how God revealed this to him, but the wealthy and powerful Abram did as he was instructed. He gathered his considerable belongings, including family and servants, and began a trek toward the place later known as the land of promise. Thus at the call of God, Abram left the circle of his friends, the region where he had power and authority, and began to make his way through desert and mountain to a destination chosen for him by the Almighty. This is what transforms Abram into Abraham and makes him such a powerful example of faithfulness; he leaves the known for the unknown at the inspiration of God (see Genesis 12:1-5). The author of the New Testament book of Hebrews points to Abraham as one of the chief representatives of authentic faith and as a pattern for our own discipleship (see Hebrews 11:1-23).

As it turns out, the "land he had been promised" was not his final destination. It was a shadow of what was to come. Abraham and his people lived in tents, an abode for wanderers, because he "looked forward to the city that has foundations, whose architect and builder is God" (Hebrews 11:13-16). Later, after Abraham's death, his descendants continued to live as nomads, a lifestyle that suggested to the early church that they, too, desired "a better country, that is, a heavenly one" (Hebrews 11:9-10). Like these examples of faith, we Christians are expected to "run with perseverance the race that is set before us, looking to Jesus the pioneer and perfecter of our faith" (Hebrews 12:1-2). By keeping our eyes on the Lord we will not "grow weary or lose heart," for the journey is long and the obstacles are many (Hebrews 12:3). As a final word, the Hebrews writer urges us to bear up under what suffering may come to us as a result of our faith because "here we have no lasting city, but we are looking for the city that is to come" (Hebrews 13:14). As people of faith we are on our way to God, not to death.

This notion of spirituality as a journey is important for a Christian understanding of life and history. Our spiritual life is actually a history within history. Our life of faith consists of the hidden saving activity of God within the more obvious aspects of what is happening around us.

As Christians we are aware that God loves us and is actively working for our good. Called as we are to a life of faith, we believe that whatever our circumstances, good or bad from human judgment, God is active in them and is using them to bring us into the kingdom. As such, life is not lived in its fullness on the level of the obvious. We weave our way through the hidden will of God so that all our journey becomes a journey home.

The Expanding Love of God

A common refrain throughout our study has been that of love. God's love is the motivating force for our creation and redemption. That love also shows itself in human nature and in human relationships. Wherever we see a person growing in the ability to receive and give love we see glimpses of the divine nature. And we believe, with Wesley, that the most visible form of God's love is seen in Jesus Christ. In Christ we participate in God's love in a far deeper way than we could without him. Jesus enables us not only to receive love from God — a love we do not deserve by any human standard, but to give love as well, and to give it most to those who deserve it least. Because we receive love as a gift from Christ, we give it to others as his gift to them — truly Christ is loving through us.

The Christian's goal, therefore, is to be increasingly open to the inrush of divine love. This love is what Wesley calls simply "the life of God in the soul of a believer." It is a "continued action of God upon the soul and a reaction of the soul upon God." God is known to us as our hearts are lifted to God, as we continually offer up

> *all the thoughts of our hearts, all the words of our tongues,*
> *all the works of our hands, all our body, soul, and spirit,*
> *to be a holy sacrifice, acceptable unto God in Christ Jesus.*[3]

Wesley was careful to relate the concept of love to the self-giving life of Jesus Christ, not to our own feelings and needs. The love Christ shares is what the New Testament calls *agape* — a love that "uniquely transcends self-centeredness in a genuine concern for the other, untainted by concerns for its consequences for the lover."[4] This definition of agape by Professor John Cobb may sound a bit formal, but it is very accurate. Looking at love this way enables us to see clearly what the cross of Christ was about: Jesus giving himself totally, without regard for his own pain and humiliation. Such love makes no demands before it acts. Jesus did not say to his disciples, "Promise me you will try to be good and then I will die for you." His love is not a matter of "I'll scratch your back and you scratch mine." It is, as Wesley said, loving God for God's own sake, not for what he could get from God, and loving others for God's sake, not because they liked him in return.[5]

As much as I respect Becker's work, I am saddened that his naturalistic approach to reality led him to conclude that human life is not embraced by a divine love. I have known persons of science

who have come to the opposite conclusion: that God exists as
Creator and Lover. I agree with Becker that we often frame
elaborate schemes of self-denial in an attempt to give our lives false
meaning, but against him, I believe God's love enables us to face the
sometimes dreadful truth about ourselves that drives us almost to
distraction. The love of God enables us to grow in the richness of
God's love despite our otherwise overwhelming limitations and
defenses. This is what Wesley meant when he emphasized that we
can grow more and more in likeness to Christ, that love can mature
and pay rich dividends we never expected. Wesley went so far as to
use the word *perfect* to describe this love. Charles Wesley put it this
way in the second stanza of a hymn of prayer:

> *Make our earthly souls a field*
> *Which God delights to bless;*
> *Let us in due season yield*
> *The fruits of righteousness;*
> *Make us trees of paradise,*
> *Which more and more thy praise may show,*
> *Deeper sink, and higher rise,*
> *And to perfection grow.*[6]

THE RHYTHMS OF GROWTH

The Apostle Paul used the phrase "in Christ" as one way to describe the intimate relationship Christians have with the Lord. To
be "in Christ" is both a gift and a mystery. It means we are hooked
by the gospel; that the good news is taking over our lives and that is
exactly what we want it to do.

The biblical passage central to this thought of Wesley's is
Romans 12:1-2:

> *I appeal to you, therefore, brothers and sisters, by the mercies*
> *of God, to present your bodies as a living sacrifice, holy and*
> *acceptable to God, which is your spiritual worship. Do not be*
> *conformed to this world, but be transformed by the renewing of*
> *your minds, so that you may discern what is the will of God —*
> *what is good and acceptable and perfect.*

These verses begin the concluding section of Paul's letter to the
Romans (12:1-15:13), a section describing the new life Christians
have in Christ. It speaks of ethics; that is, how Christians are to live

in the world. In language familiar to his audience, the great apostle says the Christian life is basically a sacrifice offered to God, a sacrifice that is living and acceptable. In Christ we belong to God; we are laid on the altar, so to speak, not as a dead animal but as a surrendered living offering, one dedicated to divine service and therefore wholly pleasing to the Almighty. Paul expects us *to become in reality* what we *already are in faith*: living offerings daily given anew to God in order to be completely changed in heart and life. I call this process of transformation the rhythm of growth.

For Wesley this process can best be understood as growing through "the means of grace." In a sermon by that title, Wesley said that God uses certain experiences and ceremonies to share grace with us — certain means of grace.[7] In his helpful book on Wesley's view of the sacraments, Bishop Ole Börgen says the means of grace are sacramental in nature and are aids to help us experience more of God.[8] (By sacramental we mean that God has given these "means" to us for our growth; they are not merely ways we thought up ourselves.)

Wesley believed that the scriptures speak of many different means of grace that God uses to strengthen us in spiritual life. Some of these include: prayer, studying the Bible, receiving Holy Communion, fasting, and sharing with other Christians. These means are not strange or mysterious, but they are special experiences in which God's love is very intense. What Wesley wanted us to know is that we should not take them for granted or regard them only as another Christian duty. When practiced in faith and love, they become powerful connectors between ourselves and God.

Wesley focused especially on three means of grace which he dubbed the "chief means."[9] They are:

Prayer. By example and teaching, Jesus showed his disciples how central prayer was to their growth in love. Wesley made prayer a very important part of his daily activity. He was so busy he had to rise very early in order to begin the day with God; but he did it, not as an obligation but as an opportunity to share himself, his joys and needs, with God. He encouraged his followers to participate in the established hours for prayer, to participate in worship (which itself is a form of prayer), and to pray each day in private.

Bible Study. Wesley liked to call this "searching the scriptures." He often called himself a "man of one book," in spite of the fact that he was well read in a number of disciplines and an author himself.

The one book he cherished was the Bible. Wesley believed that if we would read and meditate on the scriptures, we would surely grow in mature faith. The Christian life is the process of growing to maturity in Christ, and we cannot expect this to happen if we are not thoroughly grounded in the sacred text.

Holy Communion. A Christian not only prays and cherishes the scripture, a Christian also takes every opportunity to receive Holy Communion or the Lord's Supper. We believe that Christ is uniquely present in the sacrament. When taken with an attitude of repentance and faith, Holy Communion conveys spiritual grace to our lives, what Wesley called "righteousness and peace and joy in the Holy Spirit" (from Romans 14:17).

These are the major rhythms of growth for the people of God: prayer, Bible study, and Holy Communion. If utilized in faith they become more than mere routine because of the interplay they provide between ourselves and God. Even when we may feel listless and the liturgy seems dry, the mystery of God still flows through them if we are earnest in love and hope.

METHODISTS: A GROWING PEOPLE

The Anglican *Book of Common Prayer* was a trusty standby for John Wesley. Not only did it contain the major aspects of the church's ritual but also spiritual helps for private devotion. One of the prayers in the *Book of Common Prayer* is designed to be used at a funeral, as a commendation of the departed to God, with the hope that the person will be received "into the blessed rest of everlasting peace, and into the glorious company of the saints in light."[10] It reads:

> You only are immortal, the creator and maker of mankind; and we are mortal, formed of the earth, and to earth shall we return. For so did you ordain when you created me, saying, "You are dust"; yet even at the grave we make our song: Alleluia, alleluia, alleluia.

This prayer reflects Wesley's confidence that growth in likeness to God is not confined to this life. We say "alleluia" at the grave not because earthly life is finished but because fullness of life calls us forward. Our present growth is real, but it is not complete. For Wesley, as for the early church, going on to perfection continues and deepens throughout eternity. The excitement of eternity will largely be in the opportunity we will have to know as we are known, to continually discover new horizons to the meaning of our being fully formed sons and daughters of the Almighty in the kingdom of God.

For Reflection and Discussion

1. Wesley taught that growing as a Christian is a matter of being restored to full and true humanity as created in the image of God. Where are your growing edges as a Christian on the way to this kind of full and true humanity?

2. If living without faith leads people to deny death by losing themselves in distractions and illusions, how has faith enabled you to become less "illusioned" (more realistic) about life and death?

3. The major means of grace — prayer, Bible study, and Holy Communion — are all very different from one another. Why is it important for Christians to receive and experience the grace of God in so many different ways?

4. Christians believe in life after death, but they also believe in life and growth before death. How do you explain the relationship for Christians between affirming life in this world and hoping for life in the world to come?

Nine

WITNESS

The risen Christ addressed his disciples,

". . . you will receive power when the Holy Spirit has come upon you; and you will be my witnesses in Jerusalem, in all Judea and Samaria, and to the ends of the earth" (Acts 1:9).

And following these words he was taken out of their sight.

To be Christ's witness was the apostolic vocation. Later, in Acts 4:33, we read, "With great power the apostles gave their testimony to the resurrection of the Lord Jesus, and great grace was upon them all." The testimony of the Apostles consisted of more than just reporting what had happened in the past — it included an interpretation of what was happening in the present and future. They had seen the risen Christ and told others about him. For that they suffered. This suffering became another mark of the authentic disciple, as we see in Acts 22:20 where the martyred Stephen is called a witness. Thus, those who obeyed the Lord and witnessed to their faith were later cited by the author of Hebrews as a "cloud of witnesses" to inspire the church to live faithfully (see Hebrews 12:1).

This same calling inspired John Wesley. Interpreting the revival movement, he said that God has raised up the people called Methodist "to reform the continent, particularly the church, and to spread scriptural holiness over the land."[1] How was this to happen? By the same Spirit who moved the church of the Apostles, by the strength of their convictions, and by a reckless willingness to preach the living Christ! As an evangelist John Wesley had no choice. The church must bear witness if it is to be the church, the called-out ones. The church must proclaim Christ, not to cause trouble but because it can do no less. The church's nature is to say to all who will hear: "This is what happened in history and this is what is happening to us!" As a result, people by the millions have been moved over the years to accept Christ for themselves and to be enrolled in God's great "cloud of witnesses."

A CRY OF INJUSTICE

For many people the world is not a happy place. It is a place of misery, grueling labor, disease, and early death. My wife, Ruth, joined a group from her church to go on a "working" missions trip to the country of Belize. In addition to a church in need, the group found a country struggling with political unrest and burdened with poverty. When Ruth returned home she brought with her a poem scratched on a large piece of brown paper. At one time it had been pinned to a wall. Ruth found it, crumpled up in a corner of the room in which she was working. Written by Mawldyn Davies, a child who was then approximately twelve years old, the poem had the simple title of "Foodless Children":

> *Foodless children,*
> *With stomachs puffed out,*
> *Why do you have no food to eat?*
> *Why do you beg?*
>
> *Foodless children,*
> *Suffering from starvation,*
> *Why is your skin like paper?*
> *Why do your bones poke out?*
>
> *Foodless children,*
> *Eaten up by disease,*
> *Why not see a doctor?*
> *Why not?*
>
> *Foodless children,*
> *You are so thin,*
> *Your eyes are so appealing,*
> *And you will soon be dead.*

This poem is tremendously disturbing. Does it reflect the child's own life? Or maybe what the child saw happening down the block? We will never know. All we know is that here are four stanzas of pure pain. No line of beauty or joy relieves the hammer blows of suffering. The pain begins with children begging and ends with them dying. To read it is to see them: stomachs puffed out, skin like paper, and eyes "so appealing." And behind the obvious misery of the foodless children lies the agony of helpless mothers and fathers, brothers and sisters, and, worst of all, the denials of those who could help but do nothing.

That poem could have been written this morning. It addresses conditions in many parts of today's world. It is being lived out in the slums and ghettoes of U.S. cities. The tragedy of the poem is not what it says about a few specific children, as terrible as that is, but what it says about the values of a society where this can happen and keep on happening.

One cannot study world history in this century and not be appalled at the amount of human misery caused by social customs and values. Even worse is the fact that when social evil becomes a massive force, it is much more brutal than the individual evil of its citizens. Nowhere is this more evident than when racial hatred takes over the mindset of a nation.[2] Wesley condemned slavery on the grounds that such unbridled prejudice comes from the mania of a society that will not tolerate a rival.[3] The same thing can be said of war-making[4] and ruthless competition in business.[5] Some may smile when they read that Wesley attributed human evil to the crazed working of the devil, but that is exactly what people become when their views of persons different from themselves are hateful and sadistic.

Wesley and his friends viewed themselves as reformers. They hoped to "reform the continent . . . particularly the church," and to spread love where hate ruled, charity where competition ruled, mercy where unjust law ruled, and peace where lawlessness ruled. These were not mere words; Wesley had a plan. Proclaimers of the gospel would go everywhere. Small groups would be established in which women and men could grow in faith and good works. Missions to the poor and imprisoned would be started. And through the impact of the gospel in the lives of persons high and low, Wesley honestly believed an entire social system could be changed for the better. If a person can be changed, why not a family; and if a family, why not a neighborhood; and if a neighborhood, why not a town; and if a town . . . ? If God's love is turned loose, what can stop it? For all his strong preaching, blazing away at the structures and entertainments of society, Wesley was an optimist! Change is possible if we repent and put the gospel into practice. This is optimistic preaching! And this kind of bold preaching has attracted thousands to the Methodist tradition.

THE MYSTERY OF INIQUITY

Were the evils born of human greed and fear in Wesley's day (and ours!) restricted to the world of commerce and politics, that alone would set an impressive agenda for the church. But that was not the whole story. The church itself was the target of Methodist zeal. "The Mystery of Iniquity" not only infected the common ranks of society but also entrenched itself in the church.[6] The people of God, as they had been numerous times in the past, were, in Wesley's eyes, on the brink of disaster.

In a lengthy manuscript, "A Farther Appeal to Men of Reason and Religion," Wesley asked the following rhetorical questions:

> *Do we, as a people, know God? Do we consider him as God? Do we tremble at the presence of his power? Do we revere his excellent majesty? Do we remember at all times, "God is here! He is now reading my heart . . . ?" Is this the character of us English Christians; the mark whereby we are known from the [shameless unbeliever]?*[7]

Relentlessly Wesley probed as he emphasized the idea that the church he knew was faring no better than the rebellious Israelites in the days of the ancient prophets. Unbelief seemed rampant to him and it probably was, especially in the universities. In addition many pastors were lazy, and some congregations were all but neglected. But the laity was guilty as well, said Wesley, avoiding as it did the church's teaching, profaning the Lord's Day (Sunday), misusing money without regard for the poor, taking the name of the Lord in vain, and the list went on.

Reformers are given at times to overstatement, and Wesley was no exception. There were, in fact, many fine examples of Christian faith in the established church. There were social activists whose hearts were broken over the problems of society. Wesley had allies, not the least of whom were the masses who saw in him and his small groups serious attempts to right wrongs and to live according to the gospel. All this still did not take the steam out of Wesley's efforts to infuse a dead, formal church (as he saw it) with the inspiration of living faith.[8] Neither does it mean he was insensitive to the feelings of "backsliding" Christians. Wesley did not preach judgment with glee. However he may be faulted, he cannot be charged with browbeating the church. He loved the church, identified with it, and defended its better moments. And he was aware that unless they were careful, even his beloved Methodists could become just another dead sect. The issues affecting church and society alike were too crucial, too serious, to mince words.

We can learn some important lessons today from this concern of Wesley's for the integrity of the Christian life. First, we need to recognize that there is no perfect church, although there is a church moving toward perfection. We must not be surprised or dismayed when the church breaks down. The problem is not fatal. In order to hear God say, "Well done," the church will need to watch its ways, keep obedient to the Lord's teachings, and be very patient with its people. Second, the church needs to pursue humility. Even if all of us cannot agree on the "opinions" we hold about the faith, we can agree on the "essentials," as seen in the great creeds. That is quite enough for harmony, if not unity. Third, the church needs to model Christ's compassion, especially toward the angry and the poor. Finally, the church needs to pray for living faith and do all in its power to encourage it, with gentleness, in the congregation.

PLAIN OLD CHRISTIANITY

The late United Methodist historian Albert Outler said that Wesley "was a born borrower who nevertheless put his own mark on every borrowing."[9] Reading Wesley, one quickly realizes that he felt free to range around the whole Christian tradition in developing his own understanding of what it means to be Christian. This makes for a rich seedbed of ideas, each "borrowing" being carefully stitched into the fabric of Christian wholeness or happiness in God. Looking at his sources, we see his familiarity with the Orthodox Christian East, the Roman Catholic Church, and many Protestant groups, plus a great knowledge of popular science, literature, and philosophy. But most of all, as has been noted, Wesley pored over biblical passages, comparing scripture with scripture, often in the original languages, in an attempt to learn the truth. And what did Wesley come up with? A wonderful folk theology easy to understand and apply. It was what he called "plain old Christianity," and it formed his framework for witnessing.

Wesley's basic view of the faith can be summed up in six statements:

1. ***Christian faith makes a real difference in our lives***. When we become Christian, we actually become new people in Christ. Christ changes our attitudes, behaviors, and goals. Whereas we used to try to please ourselves, now we try to please God. We used to try to use people to our own advantage; now we try to help them, especially the frustrated and powerless.

2. ***Christian faith makes us confident that God is with us***. Wesley used the biblical phrase "the witness of the Spirit" to describe how we can know that Christ is at work in us and that we are not just fooling ourselves.[10] No one knows exactly how this happens, Wesley said. We only know that it does. The living God in some intimate way touches our hearts and lives so that we have an inner certainty that God is sharing love with us.

3. ***Christian faith helps us to continually receive God's healing love***. When we become Christian, we enter into a relationship with God much the same way we enter into the physical world — as babies needing to grow. The more we grow in faith the more we discover about ourselves. Sometimes we find harmful attitudes and desires very much at work in our hearts. But the more we grow the more we are healed of our spiritual sicknesses until, by God's grace, we are completely recovered from the evil that once dominated us. Wesley strongly believed that our hearts can be drained of all evil intentions and filled with love.[11]

4. ***Christian faith provides us with spiritual support***. When God becomes our heavenly parent, the people of God — the church — becomes our spiritual family. Within the church we interact as a loving family with God and with others. The church is neither a mob nor a collection of individuals but a movement of the Spirit, a movement of persons committed to one another.[12] This becomes the basis of our sense of support and care.

5. ***Christian faith is everyone's hope***. Wesley believed that society (the "world" as he called it) has turned away from God and is in many ways set against God's love. But, he also believed that God has put eternity in everyone's heart. The deeper truth is that creation is good, and people are created in God's image. It is just a matter of getting the right message to people at the right time. God has given enough grace to everyone to enable persons to choose the gospel for themselves.[13] So let us bear witness to our family, friends, and contacts. The hope we have found in Christ is their hope, too.

6. *Christian faith points us toward our destiny*. The Christian vision of the future greatly modifies the tensions of our present life. For Christians, heaven is the glorious end to a life of faith. It is God's gift to those who have run well, who have "fought the good fight," who have allowed the grace of God to flourish. Hell is another matter, one that troubled Wesley and ought to trouble us. On the brighter side, the destiny of the church is to live in the kingdom of God's glory.

My favorite Wesley verse is the last stanza of a hymn in the collection "For Believers Saved." It is a prayer, as many of Charles Wesley's hymns are. It begins by asking God to receive us — "spirit, soul and flesh" — as a living sacrifice. The rest of the hymn is a petition for God to accept and clothe our skimpy spiritual frame with God's distinctive grace. The hymn ends with a call to arms. It is the perfect way to show the importance of the Methodist witness to the thankful heart:

> Lord, arm me with thy Spirit's might,
> Since I am called by thy great name;
> In thee let all my thoughts unite,
> Of all my works be thou the aim;
> Thy love attend me all my days,
> And my sole business be thy praise.[16]

METHODISTS: A WITNESSING PEOPLE

To live for the glory of God is to witness to the glory of God. This every Christian can do. An old story tells about a young novice who kept asking Francis of Assisi to go with him into a nearby town to preach. Finally the saintly Francis agreed to the young man's demands, and the two of them set out on their mission. They entered the town's busy main street, walked its length to the far side of town, turned around and walked back. They passed stores busy with customers, women carrying goods and children playing, now for the second time, and began making their way back to their small monastery. Finally the novice could not hold it in any longer. "Father Francis," he sputtered, "I thought we were going into town to preach!" "We did, my son," Francis answered, "we did." Just living as a Christian is to proclaim the gospel!

Wesley used Colossians 3:12-17 to describe in part the same principle that Francis followed:

> *As God's chosen ones, holy and beloved, clothe yourselves*
> *with compassion, kindness, humility, meekness, and patience.*
> *Bear with one another . . . forgive each other . . . let the peace*
> *of Christ rule in your hearts . . . teach and admonish one*
> *another . . . sing psalms, hymns . . . And whatever you do, in*
> *word or deed, do everything in the name of the Lord Jesus,*
> *giving thanks to God the Father through him.*

"Whatever you do," do it in Jesus' name, giving thanks to God.
This was the Methodist's "one rule" for living. In saying this, Wesley
was trying to get people to devote themselves untiringly to Jesus
Christ. If this happens, then God is witnessed to and glorified, whether
one is preaching or babysitting, teaching a Sunday school class or
transferring stocks and bonds in a downtown highrise. To be sure,
preaching has a special role in the church, but it is not the only way
to bear witness to Christ. The person who returns excess change to
the clerk in the grocery store glorifies God as does the evangelist in
the stadium or the contemplative behind monastery walls.

The happy obligation to lay one's life at the feet of Christ for
human service is the privilege of every believer, no matter how new
or old that person is in the faith. Only in this many-faceted way will
the message of Christ reach every segment of society.

For Reflection and Discussion

1. People are aware more than ever today that the world is divided in many
ways along cultural, political, and religious lines. What must the church do
in order to bear faithful witness to Christ in this world?

2. Wesley emphasized the importance of both word and deed in making an
effective Christian witness. Why is one never sufficient without the other?

3. In what ways would you say that the deeds of the church today are most
effective in supporting the message of the gospel? In what ways are they
most detrimental?

4. Wesley believed that human beings — though fallen and infected by sin —
are nonetheless good in their deepest reality because they bear the image
of God from creation. How do you think this double-sided perspective on
human life should affect the way we approach the task of witnessing to
others?

5. What, if anything, would have to change in your thinking in order for you to
see every part of life, every area of experience, as a potential avenue of
Christian witness?

Ten

FAITHFULNESS

As she walked down the aisle of the church, Dorothy did not dream of one day running down the hallway of her home, blinded by hot smoke. Repeating after the pastor, "for better, for worse," she could not have imagined frantically pulling two of her children from the inferno and darting back into the blazing house for the third. Listening to her husband whisper, "I love you" was light years away from straining to hear a weak cry as the fire crackled in her ears. Throwing her bouquet over her shoulder to eager bridesmaids, she laughed; gasping for breath in the hallway, she cried. There was no way on her wedding day Dorothy could have foreseen that she would become a symbol of motherhood at its most demanding; that she would be an illustration of steadfast love. No one would have blamed her had she not gone back for the third child. It was useless anyway. Yet greater than giving birth to those children was Dorothy's self-sacrifice so that at least two of them might live. Such love is spontaneous, unthinking. It comes with the territory when one means the vows one takes. She was faithful when things were better; she was faithful when things were worse.

Self-sacrificing love is all-consuming. Self-sacrificing love takes great risks. Self-sacrificing love is rare. "No one has greater love than this," Jesus told the Twelve, "than to lay down one's life for one's friends" (John 15:13). The disciples understood the kind of love Jesus was talking about. They knew there were no limits to true love. But Jesus was trying to take his disciples to another level in understanding love. He was explaining to them the depth of his love for them! He said, "You are my friends if you do what I command you" (John 15:14). As God had loved Israel with a protecting, caring, covenant love, so did Jesus love his disciples. And they, in their turn, were expected to be faithful in love for God and others. They were to mirror in their lives the steadfast love of the new covenant. So it is with all of us in the church when the reckless love of God takes root in our lives.

GOD'S STEADFAST LOVE

No biblical book celebrates the perfections of God more than the Psalms. This collection of Israel's poetry extols God as worthy of adoration, as the majestic king, as the champion of the people's rights, as unparalleled in power, and as having steadfast love. It is, therefore, no surprise that the psalms conclude with a series of hallelujah songs — psalms that praise God's mercy and surpassing greatness from "the heights" and in "the earth." So awesome is the God of Israel that it is fitting for "everything that breathes" to praise the Lord. The Lord alone "reigns forever" and "executes justice for the oppressed." Before the Lord, sun and moon, angels and terrible sea-monsters, rejoice and dance. Young men and maidens, old and young together, praise the name of God, for God is perfect in relationships with people. God's word can be trusted. God's faithfulness endures forever.

> . . . the LORD takes pleasure in
> those who fear him,
> in those who hope in his
> steadfast love (Psalm 147:11).

The term *steadfast love*, occurring 127 times in the psalter, means a love that does not waver, that is made real by what it does (as in signs and wonders), and is so marvelous that it becomes the basis for absolute trust. Many Christians are familiar with the exuberant words of the psalmist as he urges all people to

> Make a joyful noise to the LORD,
> all the earth;
> break forth into joyous song
> and sing praises (Psalm 98:4).

The reason for this call to collective praise rests entirely on God's faithfulness.

> The LORD has made known his victory;
> he has revealed his vindication
> in the sight of the nations.
> He has remembered his steadfast
> love and faithfulness
> to the house of Israel.
> All the ends of the earth
> have seen the victory of our God (Psalm 98:2-3).

What victory is this? God's plan of salvation revealed through the nation of Israel for the whole world! This is the divine mission God gave to the Hebrews, a mission to proclaim the greatness of the Lord and to be a people who reflect the kingship of the Almighty.

The central feature of God's steadfast love is the covenant. This is no mere legal code carved in stone; it is rather a relationship of mutual love. This love is seen in the marriage bond, which became "the supreme demonstration of God's attitude toward Israel."[1]

Later Hosea the prophet vividly described the depth of this love of God. The prophet's faithless wife, Gomer, personifies Israel's faithlessness. She sleeps around, bears two illegitimate children, scorns her husband, and brings him public disgrace. Yet the prophet, representing the Most High God, loves his wife in spite of her behavior, pursues her, and buys her back as she stands on the auction-block, beaten down and rejected by her lovers. This is how God loves Israel. As spurned Lover the Lord yearns for reconciliation. All faithless people need do is turn from their faithlessness, and speaking words of repentance, come back to God's open arms. God has promised, "I will heal their disloyalty; I will love them freely" (Hosea 14:4).

The New Testament also gives us the message that God's faithful love is being shared with people in a new way. Pregnant with Jesus, Mary visits Elizabeth and, filled with thanksgiving at the mystery of God's working in her, sings a song of praise (Luke 1:46-55). "The Magnificat," as we call it, begins with Mary's gratitude. "My soul magnifies the Lord" (verse 47), for God was showing mercy to her. Then she utters a series of announcements: God is breaking the power of the proud and lifting up the powerless and oppressed. Likewise God is filling the poor with good things and is sending the greedy rich away with nothing. All of this is being done as a fulfillment of an old promise to Abraham. This promise has at long last come true in the son she bears. Not yet born, this unusual babe will carry the regal authority of the Messiah, the one who will sit on "David's throne." The whole life and ministry of Jesus is lived as a divine promise fulfilled; the steadfast love of God has entered history and changed it forever!

LOVE, NOT LAW

The God of steadfast love calls out a people who will respond with steadfast love. The faithfulness of God produces a people distinguished by their faithfulness. We exhibit our faithfulness in our actions, of course, but actions cannot be divorced from intention. We will not become mistake-free; but whatever we do, whether we actually do it right or not, we will do it out of a heart that loves God.

The point is, our relationship with God is one of mutual love, not unfeeling adherence to some code of law. If we looked at "The Character of a Methodist" as something against which we must be measured, we would soon give up. No one can live the life portrayed in Wesley's tract. Wesley did not intend for us to take it that way. He knew that the only way the Christian life can be lived is on the basis of love. This is precisely what our Lord said: Right standing before God is based on love for God and love for others. If we sincerely intend to do right, our efforts will be accepted as being right. This is one vast difference between living in the Spirit and living in the world. The world looks on what we produce, our God on what we sincerely intend.

The section on "happiness" that opened our study contains the correct premise for our life in Christ. We are happy because, and only because, we have come to experience God in our lives. We have discovered love! Think of it, the great God of the universe, the God of Abraham, Isaac, and Jacob; the God of Sarah, Deborah, and Elizabeth; the God and Father of our Lord Jesus Christ, captures you and me by the most unbelievable kind of self-giving love. This love went to the cross; this love said to a dying thief — who had absolutely nothing to offer — "today you will be with me in paradise" (Luke 23:43). This love seeks out a responding love. As Jesus tells us in the parable of the laborers in the vineyard (Matthew 20:1-16), it does not matter to the master at what time the workers come to toil in the fields. They all get the same pay! And this love is happy that they all get the same pay. Surely there are great benefits from having loved God from one's youth, but love rejoices whenever anyone comes to know God's love, young or old. The important thing is that love triumphs!

STANDING FIRM

What role can "The Character of a Methodist" play in a Christian's life? Like the law in the Old Testament, it can instruct us in righteousness. We need instruction. By instruction I mean learning about "the gracious expression of God's will in our lives."[2] Such instruction illuminates the path we try to follow in our quest for God. It is not a mere legal code against which we are judged, as the Torah (the Law) unfortunately became. Jesus tried to correct this misuse of God's word by teaching that true discipleship consists in loving God and others (see Matthew 22:34-40) and following him (faithfully, every day) (see Luke 9:23). Jesus thereby reinstates the original intent of the Law, to be the gracious instruction of the God who loves. In fact, love itself is "a safeguard" against every form of spiritual legalism.[3]

Wesley certainly did not want to add to the paranoia many Christians experience. For example, a good friend of mine worked hard to raise the level of his contribution to the work of the church. Eventually he was giving close to 20 percent of his income. But he did not earn a great deal of money, and he could not maintain that high level of giving and still care for the needs of his family. For a while he depended on his parents to buy shoes for his children. When I asked him why he did not cut back a little, at least until his salary was raised, he told me he was afraid. He feared God would take the money from him in other ways — through an accident or some kind of tragedy. His giving had become a fetish, a way to avoid disaster! Was he happy? Not a bit! My friend was miserable because he lived with a legalism enforced by fear. Understood this way, it is no wonder some people want nothing to do with contemporary Christianity. Such a faith breeds anxiety rather than freedom.

I admit that a close reading of Wesley's works might lead us to become over-scrupulous if the idea of salvation *by faith* and living *by love* are not held firmly in mind. Wesley quoted from Philippians 4:8 when illustrating the proper way to interpret his emphasis on living right:

> *Finally, beloved, whatever is true, whatever is honorable, whatever is just, whatever is pure, whatever is pleasing, whatever is commendable, if there is any excellence, and if there is anything worthy of praise, think about these things (Philippians 4:8).*

In the verses that precede this passage, the Apostle Paul urges his readers to "stand firm in the Lord." As he concludes the letter, he gives some practical advice on how to stand firm in the faith and how to be thoroughly united in Christ:

1. Make every effort to live in harmony with one another (verse 2).
2. Learn to rejoice in the Lord (as opposed to looking for happiness in cultural values, verse 4).

3. Be gracious and patient toward others (verse 5).
4. Do not be unduly worried about how things are going to turn out. Instead, pray (verse 6).
5. Focus on what is praiseworthy in life (verse 8).

This is the heart of Philippians 4:8! Note the context in which it sits, a context of encouragement on standing firm. There is a promise attached to those who make such efforts: "The peace of God will be with you" (verse 9*b*).

John Wesley wanted the same thing for his readers: a life faithful to the steadfast love of God. By focusing on what is praiseworthy, a Christian can do what God expects. And what God expects will benefit everyone.

FAITH UNDER FIRE

Hans-Joachim Kraus, an expert on the psalms, says the psalms teach that the person who lives an upright life will be tested by opposition and temptation.[4] John Wesley would agree. In his sermon, "Heaviness Through Manifold Temptations," he said the grief Christians suffer, particularly through sickness, tempts them to doubt the goodness of God.[5] No one, even those closest to God, can live free of temptation and suffering. This realization itself has been a trial to many people, myself included. Who does not want to be free of troubling thoughts, pressures from others, the pains of old age. Yet there they are. But if the Lord himself suffered opposition and temptation during his unique life, how can we possibly escape them, seeing the servant is not greater than the master (Matthew 10:24-25)? It helps to remember that God is for us and that God's word of acceptance at the end is what finally counts.

"The Character" was written at a time of rising opposition to the early Methodists, yet its mood is positive and upbeat. This itself is evidence that Christian life can flourish in temptation. The very nature of Christian faith — centered on the self-revelation of the holy and loving God — brings out the darker elements of human nature. It is like turning on the light in a dark, musty room and watching insects, suddenly exposed by the brightness, run for cover. The only way for unrighteousness to rest easy is for it to attempt to put out the light of the gospel.[6] Opposition and temptation put serious meaning into Christian faithfulness.

Are you tried in the fire? Has illness or a handicapping condition brought on doubts about God's love for you? Have evil thoughts risen up from your past to threaten your spiritual happiness in God? Have you been the target of some form of outright opposition? Are you frustrated because, try as you might, nothing seems to come out right? Have you suffered some deep psychological wound? Does your personality cause your intentions to be misread? If so, Wesley's writings encourage you to be brave. God is with you and will help you. The Apostle Paul uplifts us with this insight:

> No testing has overtaken you that is not common to everyone. God is faithful, and he will not let you be tested beyond your strength, but with the testing he will also provide the way out so you may be able to endure it (1 Corinthians 10:13).

How does God help us? God makes "a way out," Wesley said, by removing the temptation from us or by taking away the "bitterness" of it. (We may be saved *from* temptation or *in* it.) We should never fall because of temptation. It may disturb us — indeed it will; but it need never conquer us. Consequently, we should always be on guard so that when temptation comes, as it will, we can pray and receive divine aid. Our situation is not unique; we are not bound to go under because of what we are facing. God will not abandon us. "If God is for us, who is against us?" (Romans 8:31*b*). Christ died for us, Wesley said, and therefore nothing can separate us from Christ's love.[7] We can be faithful to the end!

METHODISTS: A FAITHFUL PEOPLE

After a long discussion on the meaning of Christ's resurrection, the Apostle Paul concluded his first letter to the Corinthians with an exhortation to faithfulness:

> Therefore, my beloved, be steadfast, immovable, always excelling in the work of the Lord, because you know that in the Lord your labor is not in vain (1 Corinthians 15:58).

Wesley wrote, "Let us endeavor, by cultivating holiness in all its branches, to maintain this hope in its full energy."[8] If we do what Wesley urged, we will not fail to fulfill the great destiny designed by God for us: eternal life in the kingdom of glory itself. The reward of faithfulness is nothing less than the eternal God, the God who in Christ set us on our journey, protected us from defeat, and finally brought us into the land of eternal day. What better end to our study than this, that all of our earthly life should at the last be crowned with glory and light. And in that setting, with all those whose hope has been wrapped up in the Lord Jesus, to join the lofty song,

> *Rejoice evermore*
> *With angels above,*
> *In Jesus' power*
> *In Jesus' love;*
> *With glad exultation*
> *Your triumph proclaim,*
> *Ascribing salvation*
> *To God and the Lamb.*[9]

For Reflection and Discussion

1. Why is it important for Christians to remember that their faithfulness will be tested by temptation and opposition?

2. People respond to pain and suffering in very different ways — anger, resignation, fear, courage, despair, faith. Why do you think some people are better able than others to bear and even to overcome pain, suffering, and tragedy?

3. When in your life have you been tempted to doubt that the steadfast love of God really applied to you?

4. Faithfulness is a matter both of outward action and of inward intention. Why is it important that these two never become separated in the way we think and talk about faithfulness?

CONCLUSION

In the Bible both Jews and Christians are called to remember the steadfast love and wonder-working power that God displayed in the history of their ancestors. The reason for giving attention to the past was to encourage the faithful to believe God could and would act redemptively in the present. Thus, the Hebrews writer wants readers to remember that "Jesus Christ is the same yesterday and today and forever" (Hebrews 13:8). The clear teaching is that God can be depended on to consistently and eternally love God's followers and act on their behalf. Indeed, Christians continue to read the Bible devotionally to be reminded by the writers of sacred scripture what God has done and, by extension, what God can reasonably be expected to do today.

This is also why the contemporary church studies John Wesley, Francis of Assisi, Teresa of Avila, and other religious figures of the past. We do not want to relive their experience, recapture their times, or even drag them into our century. Rather, we want to celebrate the God who moves through history with purpose, who allows that purpose to surface, and who will do wonderful things for us if we are open to them. By reading Wesley we not only reaffirm the roots of our own tradition, we begin to believe that vital faith and social holiness can be experienced in our world. The message of history — of the Wesley brothers — is an encouragement that the mighty God can act again in the lives of faithful people and faithful churches. Perhaps Mary's song from Luke 1:47 and 50 will become our song:

> *"My soul magnifies the Lord,*
> *and my spirit rejoices in God my Savior . . .*
> *His mercy is for those who fear him*
> *from generation to generation."*

Therefore the dream of John Wesley for a truly Christian people continues to spawn dreams of our own, dreams of finding in God a life of purpose, love, and peace. "The Character of a Methodist" remains a rich document, full of hope and encouragement. It still has its own unique attraction, as it portrays the way a Christian responds to the gospel, the church, and the world. It affords us a link with our past and with women and men who rose above their circumstances through faith in Christ and in one another.

As I have tried to show repeatedly in the previous chapters, "The Character" was originally written of people who in many ways were victims of political and social unrest. Notwithstanding such pressures, a Methodist, in Wesley's terms, was a person who lived in the real world that was more often than not a world of bitterness, disappointment, and sorrow. The message of "The Character" was not intended as an escape from a miserable life. Quite the contrary, a Methodist was a person who had found hope in the midst of despair, courage when facing terrible odds, and confidence in a God whose designs were for the common good.

The message of "The Character" is universal and timeless. It draws us because it speaks of what Jesus Christ can do with quite ordinary people. You see, the church's dream is nothing more than the common dream of every thoughtful person. The difference is where one finds the way to realize the dream. John Wesley calls us to find that reality in the risen Lord.

Peace to you!

ENDNOTES

One: HAPPINESS

[1]Earnest Becker, *The Birth and Death of Meaning*, Second Edition (New York: The Free Press, 1971), p. 122.

[2]Albert Outler (ed.), "Sermons," from *The Works of John Wesley* (Nashville: Abingdon Press, 1984), Vol. I, p. 474. Hereafter known as *Sermons*.

[3]*Sermons*, Vol. I, p. 204.

[4]Ibid., pp. 117-18.

[5]Frank Whaling (ed.), *John and Charles Wesley* (New York: Paulist Press, 1981), p. 112.

[6]Unless stated otherwise, all scripture quotations are from the *New Revised Standard Version of the Holy Bible* (Nashville: Thomas Nelson Publishers, 1989).

[7]John Wesley, *Explanatory Notes upon the New Testament* (London: The Epworth Press, 1958 reprint), p. 657. Hereafter known as *Notes*.

[8]Albert Camus, *The Plague* (New York: Vintage Books, 1972), p. 121.

[9]Erich Fromm, *The Anatomy of Human Destructiveness* (New York: Pawcett Crest, 1973), p. 296.

[10]*The Works of John Wesley* (Grand Rapids: Zondervan, n.d.), 1872, Vol. VII, p. 402, para #5.

[11]*Sermons*, Vol. I, p. 236.

[12]Robert C. Baldwin, *An Introduction to Philosophy through Literature* (New York: The Ronald Press Company, 1950), p. 311.

[13]John Wesley, "A Collection of Hymns for the Use of the People Called Methodists," *The Works of John Wesley*, Vol. VII (Nashville: Abingdon Press, 1989), p. 328. Hereafter known as *Hymns*.

[14]Thomas à Kempis, *The Imitation of Christ*, E. M. Blaiklock, tr. (Nashville: Thomas Nelson Publishers, 1979), p. 77.

Two: HOPE

[1]Allen Mandelbaum, tr., *The Divine Comedy of Dante Alighieri* (New York: Bantam Books, seventh printing, 1988), p. 21.

[2]Dorothy Marshall, *Eighteenth Century England* (New York: McKay, 1962), p. 243.

[3]*Notes*, p. 628.

[4]Colin Brown (ed.), *The New International Dictionary of the New Testament* (Grand Rapids: Zondervan, 1976), Vol. II, p. 241.
[5]*Sermons*, Vol. I, pp. 417-30.
[6]Ibid., p. 425.
[7]Gerald F. Hawthorne, *Philippians*, Vol. 43 of the *Word Biblical Commentary* (Waco: Word Books, 1983), p. 185.
[8]*Sermons*, Vol. III, p. 494.
[9]Ibid., p. 533.
[10]Ibid., pp. 191-92.
[11]*Sermons*, Vol. IV, pp. 49ff.
[12]*Hymns*, p. 154.

Three: PRAYER

[1]*Sermons*, Vol. I, p. 575.
[2]Brother Lawrence, *The Practice of the Presence of God*, E. M. Blaiklock, tr. (Nashville: Thomas Nelson Publishers, 1981), pp. 28-29.
[3]François Fénelon, *An Anthology of Devotional Literature*, Thomas S. Kepler, comp. (Grand Rapids: Baker Book House, 1977), p. 460.
[4]*Sermons*, Vol. I, p. 274.
[5]*Hymns*, pp. 336-37.
[6]*Notes*, pp. 550-51.
[7]Cf. *Sermons*, Vol. I, p. 577.
[8]*Notes*, p. 37; *Sermons*, Vol. I, pp. 577f.
[9]*Sermons*, Vol. I, p. 381.

Four: LOVE

[1]*Sermons*, Vol. II, p. 422.
[2]*Hymns*, pp. 196-97.
[3]Abraham J. Heschel, *The Prophets* (New York: Harper and Row, Publishers, 1962), p. 231.
[4]Donald P. McNeill et al., *Compassion* (New York: Doubleday and Company, Inc., 1982), pp. 13ff.
[5]Charles Johnson, *The Frontier Camp Meeting* (Dallas: Southern Methodist University Press, 1955), p. 200.
[6]Cf. Alan Richardson, *An Introduction to the Theology of the New Testament* (New York: Harper and Row, Publishers, 1958), pp. 29-34.
[7]*Works*, Vol. VII, pp. 137-38.
[8]Desmond Morris, *Manwatching* (New York: Henry N. Abrahams, Inc., 1977), p. 156.
[9]J. Glenn Gray, *The Warriors: Reflections on Men in Battle* (New York: Harper and Row, Publishers, 1959), pp. 132f.
[10]Cf. Jerry L. Mercer, *Jesus Christ: Sermon on the Mount* (Nashville: The United Methodist Publishing House, 1985), pp. 59-61.

[11]Dietrich Bonhoeffer, *The Cost of Discipleship* (New York: The Macmillan Company, 1970), p. 166.
[12]*Notes*, p. 42.
[13]*Sermons*, Vol. I, p. 523.
[14]Ibid., p. 117.
[15]*Sermons*, Vol. III, p. 307.

Five: GENTLENESS

[1]Robert C. Baldwin, *An Introduction to Philosophy through Literature* (New York: The Romand Press Company, 1950), p. 127.
[2]Ibid., pp. 127-28.
[3]Aldous Huxley, *The Devils of Loudon* (New York: Harper Colophon Books, 1952), p. 321.
[4]*Sermons*, Vol. I, p. 489.
[5]*Sermons*, Vol. III, pp. 423-24.
[6]Jerry L. Mercer, *Cry Joy!* (Illinois: Victor Books, 1987), pp. 43f.
[7]*Sermons*, Vol. III, pp. 522-23.
[8]Ibid., p. 202.
[9]*Sermons*, Vol. IV, p. 70.
[10]*Sermons*, Vol. I, p. 160.
[11]*Hymns*, pp. 508-09.

Six: SINCERITY

[1]*Sermons*, Vol. I, p. 307.
[2]*The Autobiography of Peter Cartwright* (New York: Abingdon Press, 1956), p. 164.
[3]Cf. *Sermons*, Vol. II, pp. 192-94.
[4]*Sermons*, Vol. III, p. 49.
[5]*Hymns*, p. 466.
[6]*Notes*, p. 676.
[7]*Sermons*, Vol. II, p. 242.
[8]Ibid., p. 13.
[9]Ibid., pp. 54-55.
[10]Colin Brown (ed.), *The New International Dictionary of the New Testament* (Grand Rapids: Zondervan, 1978), Vol. III, pp. 571f.
[11]Thomas S. Kepler (ed.), *Christian Perfection as Believed and Taught by John Wesley* (New York: The World Publishing Company, 1954), p. 66.
[12]Dietrich Bonhoeffer, *The Cost of Discipleship* (New York, The Macmillan Company, 1970), p. 169.
[13]Thomas Merton, *Life and Holiness* (New York: Image Books, 1963), p. 65.
[14]*Sermons*, Vol. III, p. 313.

Seven: OBEDIENCE

[1]Gerald G. May, *Will and Spirit* (San Francisco: Harper and Row, Publishers, 1982), pp. 5-6.
[2]*Sermons*, Vol. I, p. 584.
[3]*Sermons*, Vol. III, p. 8.
[4]Walther Eichrodt, *Theology of the Old Testament* (Philadelphia: The Westminster Press, 1961), Vol. I, p. 39.
[5]Frank Whaling (ed.), *John and Charles Wesley* (New York: Paulist Press, 1981), pp. 379-87.
[6]*Sermons*, Vol. I, p. 533-34.
[7]*Sermons*, Vol. II, pp. 89-92.
[8]*Hymns*, pp. 684-85.

Eight: GROWTH

[1]Earnest Becker, *The Denial of Death* (New York: The Free Press, 1973), pp. 268-69.
[2]_____, *Escape from Evil* (New York: The Free Press, 1975), p. 170.
[3]*Sermons*, Vol. I, p. 442.
[4]John B. Cobb, Jr., *The Structure of Christian Existence* (Philadelphia: The Westminster Press, 1967), p. 135.
[5]Cf. *Works*, Vol. VII, p. 495.
[6]*Hymns*, p. 588.
[7]*Sermons*, Vol. I, pp. 378f.
[8]Ole E. Börgen, *John Wesley on the Sacraments* (Grand Rapids: Francis Asbury Press, 1985), cf. pp. 95f.
[9]*Sermons*, Vol. I, pp. 384-90.
[10]*The Book of Common Prayer*, n.p., (The Seabury Press, 1979), p. 499.

Nine: WITNESS

[1]*Works*, Vol. VIII, p. 299.
[2]Eric Hoffer, *The True Believer* (New York: Harper and Row, Publishers, 1951), pp. 85ff.
[3]*Works*, Vol. VI, p. 345.
[4]*Works*, Vol. VII, pp. 340-41.
[5]*Sermons*, Vol. II, p. 271.
[6]See Wesley's sermon, *Sermons*, Vol. II, pp. 452-70.
[7]*Works*, Vol. VIII, p. 147.
[8]*Sermons*, Vol. III, p. 51.
[9]*Sermons*, Vol. I, pp. 55-56.
[10]Ibid., Vol. I, pp. 293-98.
[11]Thomas S. Kepler, *Christian Perfection as Believed and Taught by John Wesley* (New York: The World Publishing Company, 1954), p. 96.

[12]See *Notes*, p. 401, on verse 42.
[13]*Sermons*, Vol. II, pp. 156-57.
[14]*Hymns*, p. 595.

Ten: FAITHFULNESS

[1]Walther Eichrodt, *Theology of the Old Testament* (Philadelphia: The
    Westminster Press, 1961), Vol. I, p. 251.
[2]Hans-Joachim Kraus, *Theology of the Psalms* (Minneapolis: Augsburg
    Publishing House, 1986), p. 161.
[3]Eichrodt, *Theology of the Old Testament*, Vol. II, p. 298.
[4]Kraus, *Theology of the Psalms*, p. 154.
[5]*Sermons*, Vol. II, pp. 226f.
[6]*Sermons*, Vol. I, pp. 520f.
[7]*Notes*, p. 522, on verse 31.
[8]Ibid., p. 640, on verse 58.
[9]*Hymns*, p. 103.

Appendix A

THE CHARACTER OF A METHODIST: WESLEY'S VERSION

The abridged version which serves as the basis for this book is given here in its entirety for comparative purposes.* I have made two additions to "The Character" that may enhance its usefulness. First, I have given the paragraphs the same headings used in the chapter titles of the book. This will aid you in connecting Wesley's tract with the book's content. You may also want to compare Wesley's own words with the paraphrase in Appendix B. Second, I have noted *the more obvious* scripture references used by Wesley to support his vision of vital faith. Wesley loved to stitch together partial texts of scripture with his own words or even the words of others. This will give you something of an idea as to the importance of the Bible for John Wesley's spiritual life and work. Note also that the use of masculine pronouns was typical of the time Wesley lived.

*This text of "The Character" is based on Frank Whaling (ed.), *John and Charles Wesley* (New York: Paulist Press, 1981), pp. 303-06.

HAPPINESS

A Methodist is one who "loves the Lord his God with all his heart, with all his soul, with all his mind, and with all his strength."[1] God is the joy of his heart and the desire of his soul, which is continually crying: "Whom have I in heaven but Thee and there is none upon earth whom I desire beside Thee."[2] My God and my all! "Thou art the strength of my heart, and my portion forever."[3] He is therefore happy in God; yea, always happy, as having in Him a well of water springing up unto everlasting life[4] and overflowing his soul with peace and joy.[5] Perfect love having now cast out all fear,[6] he rejoices evermore. Yea, his joy is full, and all his bones cry out: "Blessed be the God and Father of our Lord Jesus Christ, who, according to His abundant mercy, hath begotten me again unto a living hope of an inheritance incorruptible and undefiled, reserved in heaven for me."[7]

[1]Matthew 22:37; [2]Psalm 73:25; [3]Psalm 73:26; [4]John 4:14; [5]Romans 14:17, 15:13; [6]1 John 4:18; [7]1 Peter 1:3-5 (selections from)

HOPE

And he who hath this hope, thus full of immortality, in everything giveth thanks, as knowing this (whatever it is) is the will of God in Christ Jesus concerning him.[1] From him, therefore, he cheerfully receives all, saying, "Good is the will of the Lord"[2] and whether he giveth or taketh away,[3] equally blessing the name of the Lord. Whether in ease or pain, whether in sickness or health, whether in life or death, he giveth thanks from the ground of the heart to Him who orders it for good, into whose hands he hath wholly committed his body and soul, "as into the hands of a faithful Creator."[4] He is, therefore, anxiously "careful for nothing,"[5] as having "cast all his care upon Him that careth for him,"[6] and in all things resting on Him, after making his "request known unto Him with thanksgiving."[7]

[1]1 Thessalonians 5:18; [2]Cf. Romans 12:2, Ephesians 1:5; [3]Job 1:21; [4]1 Peter 4:19; [5]Philippians 4:6*a*; [6]1 Peter 5:7; [7]Philippians 4:6*b*

PRAYER

For, indeed, he "prays without ceasing"[1]; at all times the language of his heart is this: Unto Thee is my mouth, though without a voice; and my silence speaketh unto Thee. His heart is lifted up to God at all times and in all places. In this he is never hindered, much less interrupted, by any person or thing. In retirement or company, in leisure, business, or conversation, his heart is ever with the Lord. Whether he lie down or rise up, God is in all his thoughts; he walks with God continually, having the loving eye of his soul fixed on Him, and everywhere "seeing Him that is invisible."[2]

[1]1 Thessalonians 5:17; [2]Hebrews 11:27

LOVE

And loving God, he "loves his neighbor as himself,"[1] he loves every man as his own soul. He loves his enemies,[2] yea, and the enemies of God. And if it be not in his power to "do good to them that hate him," yet he ceases not to pray for them, though they spurn his love, and still "despitefully use him, and persecute him."[3]

[1]Matthew 19:19, Mark 12:31; [2]Matthew 5:44; [3]Matthew 5:44

GENTLENESS

For he is "pure in heart."[1] Love has purified his heart from envy, malice, wrath, and every unkind temper. It has cleansed him from pride, whereof "only cometh contention,"[2] and he hath now "put on bowels of mercies, kindness, humbleness of mind, meekness, long-suffering."[3] And, indeed, all possible ground for contention, on his part, is cut off. For none can take from him what he desires, seeing he "loves not the world nor any of the things of the world,"[4] but "all his desire is unto God, and to the remembrance of His name."[5]

[1]Cf. 2 Timothy 2:22; [2]Proverbs 13:10; [3]Colossians 3:12; [4]1 John 2:15; [5]Isaiah 26:8*b*

SINCERITY

Agreeable to this his one desire is the one design of his life, namely, "to do not his own will, but the will of Him that sent him."[1] His one intention at all times and in all places is not to please himself but Him whom his soul loveth. He hath a single eye; and because his "eye is single, his whole body is full of light."[2] The whole is light, as when the bright shining of a candle doth enlighten the house.[3] God reigns alone; all that is in the soul is "holiness to the Lord."[4] There is not a motion in his heart but is according to His will. Every thought that arises points to Him and is in "obedience to the law of Christ."[5]

[1]Cf. Matthew 26:39, John 5:30; [2]Matthew 6:22 (Luke 11:34); [3]Matthew 5:15 (Luke 8:16); [4]Exodus 28:36, 39:30; [5]Cf. 2 Corinthians 10:5, Romans 8:2

OBEDIENCE

And the tree is known by its fruits.[1] For, as he loves God, so he "keeps His commandments,"[2] not only some, or most of them, but all, from the least to the greatest. He is not content to "keep the whole law and offend in one point,"[3] but has in all points "a conscience void of offense toward God and toward man."[4] Whatever God has forbidden, he avoids; whatever God has enjoined, he does. "He runs the way of God's commandments,"[5] now he hath set his heart at liberty. It is his glory and joy so to do; it is his daily crown of rejoicing to "do the will of God on earth, as it is done in heaven."[6]

[1]Matthew 7:16; [2]1 John 2:3; [3]James 2:10; [4]Acts 24:16; [5]Matthew 6:10; [6]Matthew 7:16

GROWTH

All the commandments of God he accordingly keeps, and that with all his might, for his obedience is in proportion to his love, the source from whence it flows, and, therefore, loving God with all his heart,[1] he serves Him with all his strength; he continually presents his soul and "body a living sacrifice, holy, acceptable to God,"[2] entirely and without reserve devoting himself, all he has, all he is, to His glory. All the talents he has he constantly employs according to his Master's will; every power and faculty of his soul, every member of his body.

[1]Matthew 22:37; [2]Romans 12:1

WITNESS

By consequence, "whatsoever he doeth, it is all to the glory of God."[1] In all his employments, of every kind, he not only aims at this, which is implied in having a single eye, but actually attains it; his business and refreshments, as well as his prayers, all serve to this great end. Whether he sit in the house, or walk by the way, whether he lie down or rise up, he is promoting, in all he speaks or does, the one business of his life. Whether he put on his apparel, or labor, it all tends to advance the glory of God, by peace and good will among men.[2] His one invariable rule is this: "whatsoever ye do, in word or deed, do it all in the name of the Lord Jesus, giving thanks to God, even the Father, through Him."[3]

[1]1 Corinthians 10:31; [2]Luke 2:14*b*; [3]Colossians 3:17

FAITHFULNESS

Nor do the customs of the world at all hinder his "running the race which is set before him."[1] He cannot therefore "lay up treasure upon earth,"[2] no more than he can take fire into his bosom. He cannot speak evil of his neighbor, any more than he can lie either for God or man. He cannot utter an unkind word of any one, for love keeps the door of his lips. He cannot "speak idle words; no corrupt conversation"[3] ever comes out of his mouth, as is all that is not "good to the use of edifying," not fit to "minister grace to the hearers."[4] But "whatsoever things are pure, whatsoever things are lovely, whatsoever things are" justly "of good report,"[5] he thinks, speaks, and acts "adorning the doctrine of God our Saviour in all things."[6]

[1]Hebrews 12:1; [2]Matthew 6:19; [3]Matthew 12:36, Ephesians 4:29; [4]Ephesians 4:29; [5]Philippians 4:8; [6]Titus 2:10

Appendix B

The Character of a Methodist: A Paraphrase

The following paraphrase is an attempt to let Wesley speak in a more contemporary way. Remember as you read that this was Wesley's *vision* for Methodists, not a simple statement about what all Methodists had already become.

Happiness

A Methodist is a person whose whole life centers on loving and serving God. Methodists understand that all of life's joys are expressions of God's goodness. Thus a Methodist wants to please and honor God in everything. It is natural for a Methodist's heart to sing, "Whom have I in heaven but you? And there is nothing on earth that I desire other than you. My flesh and my heart may fail, but God is the strength of my heart and my portion forever." When people feel this way about God, they yearn to share their faith with anyone who will listen.

We should not be surprised when Methodists appear to be happy. They are! They are happy because to them God is like an ever-flowing fountain, constantly pouring out radiant joy and inner peace into their hearts. In addition to this, a Methodist's heart is joyful because God increasingly replaces old fears with God's love. So a Methodist's spirit leaps for joy and gives praise to God, saying, "Give honor to the God and Father of our Lord Jesus Christ. God's great mercy has been given to me abundantly and I am God's child, both now and for the ages to come. Hallelujah!"

Hope

The person who has hope in God's gift of life, both here and hereafter, is tasting a bit of heaven on earth. So Methodists can be thankful for everything by trusting in God regardless of what happens. A Methodist takes comfort in knowing that all of life can be lived according to God's will. This means Methodists take whatever life holds, good or bad. They have learned to give thanks to God in every kind of circumstance.

It makes absolutely no difference to a Methodist whether the physical body is healthy or racked with pain. Neither does it make much difference if one has a lot of money or has none. Living zestfully or on the brink of death is not the main issue for Methodists. A Methodist can rejoice in God no matter what! This may sound strange but Methodists believe God will bring something good out of every situation. Therefore a Methodist is committed to God and feels good about that because God can be trusted to do what is best. This means Christian life can be restful, not fearful. And a Methodist's prayers are peaceful because they are made in hope and with thanksgiving.

Prayer

Methodists pray all the time. By that I mean a Methodist's heart is always tuned in to God. Confidence in God's love does not need to be broken, regardless of where Christians are or what they are doing. A Methodist's heart is always hidden in God, whether busy with people or simply resting. In fact, a Methodist thinks of God on waking in the morning and on going to bed at night. All this is one way of saying that a Methodist walks with God all the time and is, therefore, always open to the leading of the Holy Spirit. It is a true statement that a Methodist sees God everywhere!

Love

The mighty love of God working in us enables us to value others as highly as we value ourselves. And, believe it or not, this includes one's enemies! A Methodist does as much good as possible for everyone. It is true, however, that we are sometimes hindered by others in being able to show Christ's love as fully as we would like. But if that is the case, we can always pray for people, asking God to pour blessings into their lives. And don't forget, this includes those who consider themselves our enemies. Even if our enemies actually hurt us or try to harm us, we still pray sincerely for them.

GENTLENESS

A heart that is pure is so filled with God's love that deepseated attitudes such as envy, hateful thinking, and uncontrolled anger are overcome. As a result, a love-filled Methodist becomes a gentle person. We believe God's love frees us from the need to step on others in order for us to have self-respect. God enables us to respond to others with mercy, kindness, humility, simplicity, and patience. At the same time, we do not need to be unduly threatened by others, since no one can take from us what we value most: the loving presence of God. Thus, Methodists are free from the domination of negative social values, especially prejudices that divide people from one another.

SINCERITY

A sincere Methodist not only studies sacred scripture but looks for ways to put into practice what it teaches. A sincere Methodist not only prays to God but looks for ways to put prayers to work. A sincere Methodist does not think of God only on special occasions but tries to remember God and praise God's name all the time. A sincere Methodist believes the gospel; that is, a Methodist trusts God so much that all of life is shaped by that trust. Sincerity toward God and toward others integrates our otherwise fragmented lives.

OBEDIENCE

A Methodist's depth of commitment is as obvious as ripe fruit on a good tree. A Methodist's "good fruit" comes from a good conscience. This means a Methodist tries to be whatever God expects a Christian to be. Whenever one is "in Christ," that person wants to give 100 percent to the Lord, not just 99 percent. So whatever seems to displease God, a Methodist leaves alone. On the other hand, whatever pleases God, that is exactly what a Methodist wants to do. Methodists know that when our hearts are set free by God's love, then a desire to please God springs up in the heart like water from a well! A Methodist's highest joy is to do God's will all the time, just as it is being done in heaven.

GROWTH

A Methodist zealously keeps God's commandments. This means that Methodists eagerly and with strong determination want to live out the implications of God's love in their lives. We know that anyone who loves God supremely wants to serve God in every acceptable way. We say a Methodist's pride and joy is to be a "living sacrifice," holy and acceptable to God; that is, to be totally yielded to God's will, placing every natural talent and spiritual gift at God's disposal.

WITNESS

Whatever a Methodist does is a witness to God's glory. At the risk of repeating myself unnecessarily, I want to say again: Methodists try to live in ways that bring glory to God. Whether at work or play, a Methodist has a "single eye" in serving God. It is not stretching things too far to say that our business life is the same as our prayer life. Literally every thing and every relationship is given to God. Methodists believe honoring God is the one business of our lives. We are God's compassionate witnesses even when we are at a party! I cannot say it strongly enough: In every detail of our lives we glorify God by being people of goodwill and peace. Our one rule for life is, "Whatever I do or say, I will do it in the name of the Lord Jesus Christ, and I will always be grateful to God."

FAITHFULNESS

It is important to note that a Methodist's zeal for new life in God is not determined solely by the values of society. For example, a Methodist will not hoard money if it hurts someone else. Likewise, Methodists will not deliberately say hurtful or embarrassing things about someone else. The love of God in a Methodist's heart keeps him or her from behaving like this. A Methodist also avoids gossip like the plague! We can take this one step farther by saying Methodists abstain from all questionable talk — talk that does not build others up in the grace of the Lord. A Methodist always listens to Paul's advice: "Whatever is pure, lovely, just, and holy" is what we should give ourselves to at all times.

This is the character of a Methodist!

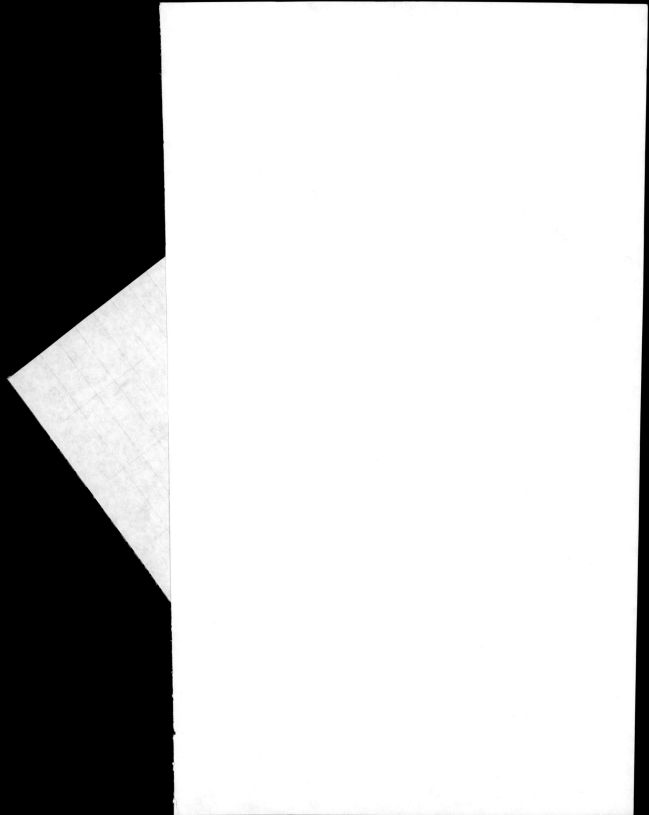

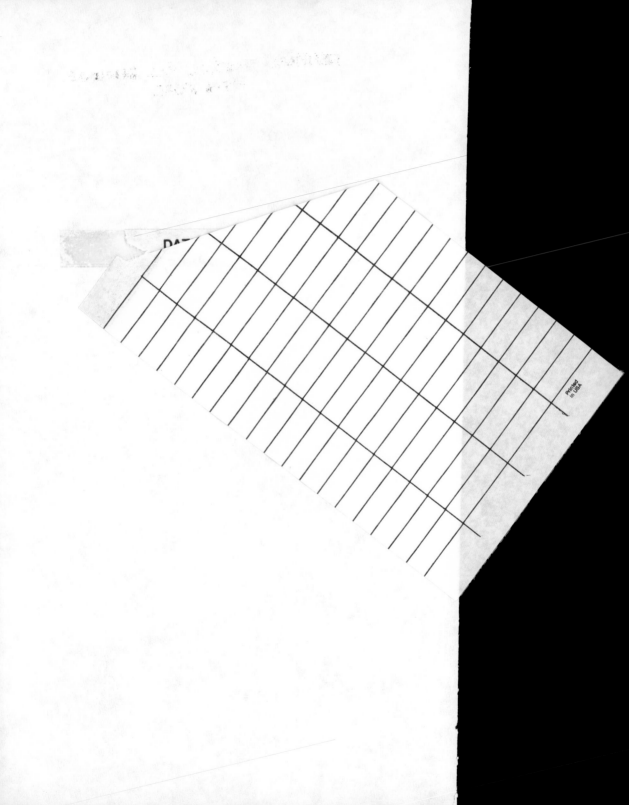